The Financial Times Essential Guide to
Negotiations

The Financial Times Essential Guide to Negotiations

How to achieve win–win outcomes

Geof Cox

PEARSON

Harlow, England • London • New York • Boston • San Francisco • Toronto • Sydney
Auckland • Singapore • Hong Kong • Tokyo • Seoul • Taipei • New Delhi
Cape Town • São Paulo • Mexico City • Madrid • Amsterdam • Munich • Paris • Milan

Pearson Education Limited
Edinburgh Gate
Harlow
Essex CM20 2JE
England

and Associated Companies throughout the world

Visit us on the World Wide Web at:
www.pearson.com/uk

First published 2012

© Geof Cox 2012

Pearson Education is not responsible for the content of third-party internet sites.

ISBN: 978-0-273-77221-7

British Library Cataloguing-in-Publication Data
A catalogue record for this book is available from the British Library

Library of Congress Cataloging-in-Publication Data
A catalog record for this book is available from the Library of Congress

10 9 8 7 6 5 4 3 2 1
16 15 14 13 12

Typeset in 8.75/12pt Stone serif by 30
Printed and bound by Ashford Colour Press Ltd., Gosport

Contents

Introduction

Life is a series of negotiations

My colleague Jem Scanlan describes life (in an article on project management) as being a series of projects, and suggests the following equation:[1]

$$L = \sum P^i, \text{ from } i = 1 \text{ to n, where } L = \text{Life and } P = \text{Project}$$

I like to think that life is also a series of negotiations. Every day, every hour in a day, we are negotiating something. Negotiation skills are not just limited to those headline grabbing issues that fill the world news headlines: peace treaties, environmental protection, climate change, hostage release, ransom demands, trade union disputes, strikes, planning regulations, political coalitions, etc. These are situations that few will encounter at first hand. But you will use the same, basic negotiation skills when you are planning a work schedule, managing a project, agreeing priorities with a colleague, finalising a deal with a supplier, setting a deadline, responding to a request for your input, asking for a pay increase or agreeing the price of a purchase in the market, discussing which restaurant to go to for dinner, and sorting out your holiday plans.

In these, and in any number of other situations faced on a daily basis, you want to optimise the situation in your favour, which often conflicts with the interests of the other party who wants to optimise the outcome in their favour. There is a conflict. It may not be of sufficient scale that you go to war, but there is a conflict that needs to be resolved so that both parties can move forward. You can use force and beat the other person into submission (physically or metaphorically), or you can seek to find a solution which is mutually acceptable.

---

[1] Scanlan, Jeremy (2003) 'Life Projects for 21st Century Leaders', *Organisations & People*, Vol. 10, No. 2.

In situations which are one-off (you will never meet the other person again), there is a temptation to use your power to get as large a slice of the cake as possible, at the expense of the other person. You do not concern yourself with the feelings or needs of the supplier or the market stall owner. You fight to buy what you want at the lowest price. This is successful at one level – you get a deal at the lowest price – but the potential damage to your relationship with the other party brings with it a risk if you need something from them in the future, for example if you discover at a later date that there is some problem or defect in your purchase that you need to be fixed. You may be prepared to take this risk in some circumstances, such as buying a cheap, readily available commodity. In other situations you may be more concerned about not upsetting the seller, for example if you will be using a dealer for the servicing of your computer. In these cases, you will want to put some effort into maintaining a good relationship as well as getting a good price. This is where the skills of negotiation covered in this book will help.

The win–win approach to negotiating

It is surprising that many negotiations that are conducted in the business world still use the competitive, combative approach that is typified by one person winning and the other person losing. Purchasing departments use competitive, sealed bid tenders to find a supplier at the lowest price and with the most advantageous terms and conditions of sale, only finding out when the deal has been signed that the supplier has cut so many corners in order to drive the price down that the quality and reliability of the product is compromised, and they have no interest in putting any effort into rectifying the situation. The buyer is then involved in the higher costs of putting things right and managing an antagonistic relationship, costs and difficulties which more than outweigh the savings made in the original tender, and often made even more costly by the need to use litigation to obtain any redress.

This book promotes a different approach to negotiation; an approach which will enable you to negotiate deals so that you get what you want and at the same time maintain (or even build) a positive working relationship with the other party. You can work with them again tomorrow and the next day without any fear of reprisal. This approach is commonly referred to as win–win negotiating, as compared with the competitive or positional negotiation approach which leads to one side winning and one side losing – a win–lose outcome. A win–win approach is much more suited to the twenty-first century business environment, where partnership working, outsourcing and contracting services, and complex relationships are prevalent. It is also an approach which is essential for conducting negotiations inside an organisation, where good working relationships are critical.

How this book is structured

The book is divided into three main parts. It is a practical guide that will introduce you to the skills and processes used in reaching win–win outcomes, whether you want to use these for day-to-day negotiations, or whether you want to use them in more complex situations such as labour disputes, outsourcing operations, partnership working or mediating in major conflicts. The skills and processes used in simple and complex negotiations are the same, the difference is only in the complexity and the level of skill required.

Part 1: Planning it

In Part 1, I deal with the thinking behind win–win negotiating and how you can prepare your thinking and develop your skills so that you can be successful. In Chapter 1, I make the case for a win–win approach to negotiation in organisations, and how to deal positively with the conflicts that exist. Chapter 2 focuses on the benefits of collaborative negotiation, and the impact of different approaches to negotiation. Chapter 3 introduces the key phases of the negotiation process with checklists and guidance that help you to prepare for a negotiation, and to make a judgement on how much time and effort to put into the preparation phase. Finally in Chapter 4, I cover the communication behaviours that are essential for conducting the face-to-face elements of the negotiation.

Part 2: Doing it

There are five chapters in Part 2, which is focused on the mechanics of planning for and conducting a negotiation. Chapter 5 introduces a five-step planning guide to help you to determine what you need to do to prepare yourself before entering the negotiation arena. Chapter 6 guides you through the stages and actions in the negotiating arena when you are face to face with the other party(ies), exploring the issue and finding a mutually acceptable agreement. In Chapter 7 you can learn from the behaviour of successful negotiators – what they do and don't do. In Chapter 8, I explore the darker side of negotiating practice: the use of tactics and dirty tricks that are designed to gain the upper hand. Whilst you might not choose to use these yourself, you need to build your resistance to them if they are used by the other party. Finally, Chapter 9 looks at the application of the basic skills and processes of negotiation in more complex situations such as international and remote negotiation.

Part 3: Reviewing it

In Part 3, I provide you with a number of checklists, review questions and assessments that will help you to evaluate the quality of the negotiation that you have concluded, and identify areas where you could improve in future negotiations. Following the coaching tips and development exercises that I also include will help you to develop in those areas where you identify an opportunity for improvement, and therefore ensure even more successful outcomes in the future.

Acknowledgements

I first understood the importance of relationship building in negotiations when I worked at the 'sharp end' of industrial relations at a distribution plant for Esso Petroleum in Birmingham. It was at a time of major industrial unrest in the country and at a time when the trade unions, and therefore their local shop stewards, wielded a lot of power. Without any formal training, it seemed appropriate to me to try to find solutions to disputes that meant that both the company and the union members were happy and did not lose face. Talking seemed to be more productive than fighting, and I was reminded of Winston Churchill's words 'Jaw, jaw is better than war, war.'

Later, when I became involved with national wage negotiations between the oil industry in the UK and the trade unions (at that time it was the Transport & General Workers Union, now part of Unite), I learned that my instinctive reactions were underpinned by a major body of negotiation theory and practice. In my wider role I had the opportunity of not just helping to negotiate some landmark national deals with the union, but also to settle a number of local disputes through paying attention to both the issue and the relationship. It was this experience which then led me to take a further interest in the subject: to research, to learn more, to teach others and to consult.

Influences along my journey have included Roger Harrison and David Berlew with their work on positive influence and negotiation. The work of Roger Fisher and William Ury at the Harvard Negotiating Project was an early source of inspiration, as was the work of Chester Karrass in the USA and Gavin Kennedy in Scotland. Walt Hopkins and the late Chuck Dufault were my partners in Castle Consultants International where we developed and ran training workshops in positive and win-win negotiating across Europe, and developed a number of innovations and concepts for win–win, remote and cross cultural negotiation. I have designed and run my own workshops in negotiation and conflict management in Europe, the USA, the Middle East and in AsiaPAC, and in the process continued my learning about different approaches and negotiation cultures. In consulting with a number of multinational companies, I have helped them to conclude commercial deals, partnership agreements, and outsourcing and off-shoring arrangements that have provided long-term mutual benefit. In recent years, working with my partners in Learning Consortium, whose focus is on continuing professional development, has helped me to further understand and apply the models to myself and my work.

My colleagues have provided very helpful and insightful comments on the content. My wife Joan was especially helpful in proofreading my text and making sure that my grammar and spelling were consistent throughout. My publishing editor Christopher Cudmore of Pearson has encouraged and provided enormous support and direction throughout the process.

Finally, I must acknowledge all of the organisations and individuals who have been on the receiving end of my consulting and training in interpersonal and negotiation skills for the past 25 years. These organisations and individuals have contributed the case studies and examples which illustrate the chapters. Names and contexts have been changed to protect both the guilty and the praiseworthy, but their contribution is invaluable.

Geof Cox

Planning it

1

Why negotiation is important in organisations

We negotiate every day. We are negotiating almost all the time. We negotiate with business partners, clients, suppliers, colleagues, family members, neighbours, friends, our children's teachers, local authorities, social and professional groups. We negotiate at work, at home and in our social environment. And our success in these situations depends entirely on our understanding of the negotiation and communication process, the way in which we engage with the other parties involved, and our skills as a negotiator.

Negotiation is a vitally important skill for everyone in the workplace today. It is no longer an activity that is undertaken by a few professionals in sales, contracts departments or purchasing groups, or by labour relations specialists and lawyers. The nature of today's business means that we are all involved in negotiating in our day-to-day work activity.

Many businesses are now organised in matrix or project based structures. Businesses work across cultures and time zones. People inside organisations work in close cooperation with other departments. There is an increasing pace to working life, meaning that decisions need to be taken quickly, with limited information available. More use is being made of contractors and outsourced resources. Decision making is being pushed further down the organisation, either because it is seen to be more effective to make decisions as far down as possible, or because repeated down-sizing, 'right-sizing' and restructuring have removed the layers of management that used to make the decisions.

All of these features – and more – of the modern working environment are sources of conflict, and therefore opportunities for negotiation. If not dealt with effectively, they become sources of frustration, confusion and despair. The scenarios that most trouble attendees on the workshops I run on influencing, negotiating and conflict management are issues that are internal to their organisations.

Working positively with conflict

Sources of conflict

Sources of conflict can be traced to an objective or more psychological cause (see Figure 1.1). Objective conflict is rooted in organisation structures such as the matrix which shows up conflicts between its axes; in company policies and directives; in the competition for limited resources; in the decision-making process; in unclear objectives; in differences between manager and individual expectations; and in different processes and systems. Psychological causes include: differences in personal values and beliefs; cultural background; behaviour; lack of clarity of role; difficult relationships; and personal sensitivity.

Objective	Psychological
• Organisation structure	• Cultural background
• Company policies, directives, instructions	• Personal values and beliefs
• Constant change	• Skills and behaviours
• Competing for resources	• Working or personal stress
• Decision-making process	• Clarity of role
• Unclear mission or objectives	• Relationships
• Manager's expectations	• Personal sensitivities
• Processes and systems	

figure 1.1   Sources of conflict

Whatever the cause, the outcome can be traumatic, negative and unproductive. More energy is often expended on fighting battles inside organisations than fighting the competition outside. Game play predominates, people try to win at the other department or team's expense, they deliberately withhold or distort information, they pursue their own goals at the expense of the bigger picture, and make exaggerated claims about their own performance relative to others.

Example

A recent story illustrates this game play. A salesman had responsibility for the lead negotiation with a multinational client for the supply of materials. He contracted a deal with the Swiss headquarters, with the key supply location being in Germany. The material had a high transport cost, so other locations that had lower demand for the material often contracted local, more cost-effective supply agreements.

The main supply company factory then found itself in a massive overstock situation, and incentivised its sales force across Europe to move the stock, providing low prices for spot sales of the material. A saleswoman in France contacted the local office of the multinational client and sold a consignment at the spot price. This undermined the contract price by a considerable margin, so the large contract supply in Germany had to be delivered at the spot rather than the contract price, netting an overall massive reduction in the profit margin. When the supply situation returned to 'normal', not only had the margin been eroded but the trusting relationship between the salesman and the client had been compromised. The French saleswoman had met her targets, and got her bonus, but the company as a whole lost revenue.

Conflict management strategies

If the conflict itself is not bad enough, matters are often made worse as many of the strategies used to deal with it merely control the conflict, and may even legitimise and prolong it.

Trying to deal with the conflict by regulatory responses such arbitration or the imposition of new rules and procedures does not deal with the underlying issues and leaves the causes of the conflict in place to emerge again later. Competing or applying pressure from one side over the other, or trying to resolve conflict through the application of force do not work either: they create even more differences and resentment, and undermine the relationship between the parties. Such strategies create more and different conflict, often moving an objective dispute to a personal one which is much harder to resolve.

Escalating the disagreement to the next level of management may provide a solution, but it undermines the trust and respect in the initiating party which may lead to further interpersonal conflict. Arbitration may solve the presenting issue, but there are often a range of underlying concerns and conflicts that are not resolved and will erupt at a later date. Observing any major trade dispute that goes to arbitration is a case in point – most of them surface again a few months or years later under slightly different terms, but they are essentially the same conflict.

All of these are potentially negative strategies – negative because although they may appear to resolve the dispute, they often do not (frequently making it worse) or create more conflicts in the course of the process. Positive outcomes are achieved by bringing the conflict into the open and engaging openly in dialogue with the other party or parties. To achieve a long-lasting solution to conflict, we need to confront it in an environment where collaboration is possible and we can negotiate a mutually acceptable outcome, where both parties are happy – a win–win solution.

Positive and negative conflict management strategies are shown in Figure 1.2.

Positive
- Agree common objectives
- Provide information
- Provide coordination mechanisms
- Communicate openly
- Remove territorial or role conflicts
- Negotiate

Negative
- Escalate
- Arbitrate
- Impose rules/procedures
- Create intermediary position
- Confrontation
- Separation
- Neglect/avoid
- Go to war

figure 1.2   Conflict management strategies

Working in project and matrix organisations

Many people are only too well aware of working in a matrix as they are suffering the frustrations of being there:

- 'It's impossible to get any work done around here. There is always someone who has an interest even in the smallest of decisions.'
- 'I don't know what they do or how to get them involved.'
- 'I have one boss who says I should focus on X and another who says focus on Y.'
- 'No-one knows who is responsible any more.'
- 'How do I get things done when all of my team reports to a different manager?'
- 'I have the responsibility for the project completion but I don't control any of the resources.'
- 'How do I know if something is being done right when the person doing the job is in a different country and doesn't even work for our company?'
- 'The project team is located in three different continents and time zones, so that there is no time when we are all in our offices at the same time. Yet efficient communication is the key to our success. How do you make that work?'

Given these difficulties, it is hard to accept that matrix or project organisations are worth retaining. Their advantages are that they are a reflection of the complexity of the business environment which demands that organisations innovate faster and leverage their resources more effectively. The matrix, well structured and managed, improves the quality and speed of business decisions by focusing cross-functional expertise in responsive, customer facing groupings that reflect the fluid and complex environment in which the organisation operates. The project organisation allows for flexible work teams to focus on introducing change and innovation, cutting across lines of bureaucracy and functional interest.

These structures are often shown as in Figure 1.3, where the organisation is managed through two lines of command – one line based on the functions of research, manufacturing, sales and finance, and the other line based on product lines A, B and C. So someone working on Product A in Sales will have a dual reporting relationship to a sales manager responsible for overall sales and to the product manager who has the overall responsibility for the product. A project organisation structure looks very much the same, but with a project focus replacing the product focus.

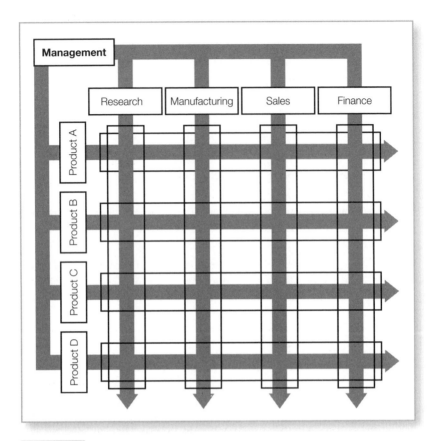

figure 1.3   A matrix organisation structure

A matrix may be drawn with respect to geography and function, or projects and functions, or even three-dimensionally (product/function/geography). The matrix may be stronger in one dimension than the other, usually depicted by having 'dotted line' relationships versus 'straight line' relationships, the straight line usually taking precedence, or they may be balanced where there is no priority. However they are drawn this is usually a reflection of the priorities and tensions that exist in the environment in which the organisation operates. For example, the engineering company reflecting the tensions between maintaining the standards and expertise in engineering and the need to deliver projects; or the fast moving consumer goods (FMCG) company reflecting the tensions between the demands of the local marketplace, the product range and the cross-functional team working to deliver the product to market.

It is the dual (and sometimes multiple) reporting relationship that leads to the frustrations and confusions that were voiced earlier by those caught up in the matrix or project net. These frustrations are the sources of conflict that need to be resolved, and are greater when people have not been adequately trained to deal with conflict, or if the matrix has been implemented badly.

When working with a company in Switzerland that was implementing a matrix structure under orders from its US parent, it took the senior executives nearly 18 months to stop fighting amongst themselves for ultimate control and find a way of getting the structure to work. 'I am Executive VP for Marketing, so I am in control of Marketing in Russia' versus 'I am Executive VP for Russia, so I am in control of Marketing in Russia' eventually became 'How do we work together to deliver a marketing operation in Russia that delivers the best value to the Company?' after they conducted an effective negotiation – but not until a lot of frustration and anger had detracted from the real objective of developing the business in Russia. In the meantime, the rest of the organisation was even more confused and frustrated.

People who work in a matrix need to recognise that the confusion and conflict they experience is deliberate. If there is clarity, then there is no need for a matrix. A matrix or project structure reflects the complexity, multiple objectives and divided loyalties that exist in the real working environment. It is designed to force communication between the matrix partners to align goals and ensure role clarity. This is the inherent strength of the matrix and the project. The corollary is that it requires highly developed skills in listening, agreement building, collaboration, negotiation and strategic thinking. It requires self-awareness to understand your impact on others. It requires skills in communicating effectively with a wide range of people from different functions and cultures, often across large distances so involving less face-to-face contact. These are skills that are not naturally present in simple hierarchies. Negotiation needs to take place at the crossover points of the axes with the objective of adding value for the organisation.

There is no one right way in a matrix; if there is, then the situation is not complex enough for a matrix structure. There is no certainty in a project, which by its nature is doing something that has not been done before. With complexity and uncertainty come tensions and options. These are not situations in which you should try to tell people what to do – this only leads to resistance, both active and passive, or a power struggle. You do not have the authority anyway, so don't try to use it. Instead, you need to grow your influence and negotiate mutually acceptable, win–win outcomes.

Working in cross-cultural situations

Example

Two car manufacturers were discussing collaboration and even a possible merger. One manufacturer was Swedish, the other French. At the initial meetings between the company boards, the Swedish team used well constructed presentations which everyone was expected to listen to, raising any discussion points at the end of the presentation. The French style was to address a question or a discussion point when it arose. So there were frequent interruptions from the French side, which were considered 'rude' by the Swedes and disrespectful to the speaker.

When it was time for the French lead speaker to take the stand, he made a brief statement to the meeting which, in France, would have stimulated the rest of the board to debate and discuss. Instead, he was greeted with silence, as the Swedish team were waiting for the detail of the presentation. The Swedish team felt affronted that the French team had not put any perceived thought or effort into preparing its position, and was itself unable to discuss and debate 'off the cuff'.

The conclusion from these initial discussions was that each company decided it could not work with the other because of cultural differences, despite the fact that they both needed a working partner to inject ideas, develop new models and share production costs in an increasingly competitive market. If they had put more effort into understanding and working with their differences, and negotiated an understanding about how to work together, then they might have concluded an important deal. Win–win negotiating is not just about the what – the issue – it is also about the how – the relationship.

Differences in culture – and therefore conflict – arise from a number of different sources, not just nationality. In the workplace, we see the growing differences in the different generation cultures of Baby Boomer, Generation X, Generation Y, and soon, Generation Z. Different professions, genders, functions, organisations, ages, nationalities and races exhibit fundamental differences in the way in which they typically behave, which can cause the same misunderstandings as between the Swedish and French car manufacturers. They have different approaches to negotiation and to interpersonal communication which need to be taken into account.

It is vitally important to get positive outcomes from these cross-cultural situations, as they are increasingly common in organisations where outsourced and offshore operations are being deployed, and the use of global project groups is growing. Business is becoming more global, and the communications technology we now use puts the world onto our desktops in real time. Instead of viewing these differences as negative or creating blockages to collaboration, as with the previous example, the differences should be welcomed and outcomes negotiated that ensure that the benefits of the diversity are achieved. What it needs is the application of our mindset of collaboration and win–win rather than the defensive and competitive routines often played out.

Working in partnerships

Another major development in the business environment that makes win–win negotiating an essential skill is the increasing use of partnership working in both the private and public sectors. In some cases in the public sector, partnership working is a pre-requisite for organisations to gain access to funding. But, as most organisations were created to serve their own values and interests, partnership working is not easy. It requires some considerable effort to negotiate common interests and goals, and to identify the way you can work together with another organisation with whom you might be in competition in other situations.

Partnership working involves getting organisations together to work for a common purpose, and setting up a structure for them to carry out this joint activity. There is usually an overarching purpose for partners to work together to achieve a range of specific objectives and address specific issues. For example, companies who rely on new product development often partner with universities to tap into the latter's research and development activities. The company gets a source of new ideas and access to fundamental research, the university gets funding and support for its academic research programme. In oil exploration and production, there is nearly always a partnership operation between companies; not just for the sharing of risk and funding, but also to enable expertise to be shared to mutual benefit. So a company with significant assets but no production expertise will partner with a company who has that expertise – one company gets its assets exploited and the other gets an opportunity to staff and operate an oil field.

In the provision of local authority services, there is a trend towards partnering with specialist agencies and the voluntary sector to provide services instead of the previous direct provision by the local authority. The local authority benefits from reduced direct costs and headcount, whilst still ensuring that its statutory responsibilities are carried out. Its partners have access to funding and opportunities to deliver the services that they are designed for.

Difficulties experienced in partnership working often stem from inadequate initial negotiating of the common goal and the mutual benefit, and the lack of ongoing negotiation on issues that arise during its operation. The key principles of partnership working are openness, trust and honesty, agreed shared goals and values, and regular communication between partners. This suggests that in order for partnerships to work there is a requirement for continuous negotiation.

Example

TNT and the World Food Programme – an effective partnership

TNT is a private sector delivery company and is a partner in the United Nations World Food Programme, which provides food aid to over 90 million people across the world each year. In 2001, the Chief Executive of TNT became aware of the horrifying number of children in the developing world dying of hunger every hour, despite there being enough food produced annually to feed the global population. He identified that TNT's core business function – logistics – was at the heart of the problem. He believed that TNT could work jointly with the United Nations World Food Programme for the benefit of those facing starvation worldwide.

TNT supports the World Food Programme through advising on the logistics of the World Food Programme; assistance with disaster management; collaboration on private sector fundraising; assistance with accounting, finance and human resources; and promoting employee volunteering. As well as the inevitable benefit of publicity, TNT also recognises that this partnership has led to other benefits, such as increased employee morale and job satisfaction, resulting in increased productivity and knowledge sharing. The World Food Programme, as well as getting a financial donation in cash and kind from TNT, gets access to the knowledge and expertise of a world-class logistics organisation which better equips it to deal with emergencies and distribution management.

Evaluation of this partnership shows that success has been due to high-level management commitment to the principles of partnership and collaboration and a clearly understood purpose, and a formal agreement with built-in review periods which prevents the partnership from continuing beyond its shelf life and also gives the opportunity to formally negotiate changes and restructuring after a suitable bedding in period. The involvement of staff at all levels in both organisations in the delivery of the partnership agreement also ensured that the goal was met and the benefit was felt by everyone. The partnership is seen to be beneficial to both sides, and is continually adapted to keep it that way.

Win–lose is not an option

The way in which work and organisation life is structured means that we have to work with conflict in real time. The complexities and tensions that exist in the world of work are delivered in real time to our desktops in emails, instant messaging, webinars, teleconferences and video links, all exhorting us to make immediate decisions and judgements in areas that have a long-reaching impact. Decision making and responsibility are pushed further down the organisation, and the growth of matrix organisation structures and project working forces us into relationships with people who are very different to us and have different priorities and objectives. Our organisations forge partnerships with other organisations to develop and deliver products and services. We are continually working with people over whom we have no formal authority, but who need to do things for us that ensure we meet our work objectives.

The way in which work is done in the twenty-first century is through effective relationships with diverse groups and individuals. In such an environment, we cannot afford to have the differences inherent in those relationships causing harmful conflict, destructive competition or fruitless argument. Strategies that lead to win–lose dialogue put long-term relationships, on which the success of our organisations depends, at severe risk. The answer is to use the differences that emerge as the source of constructive discussion, the spark for innovative solutions and the opportunity of collaboration. The answer is win–win negotiation. Win–lose is not an option.

In the next chapters, I outline the thinking behind win–win negotiation – the process structures, strategies, tactics, tools, techniques and behavioural skills that you can use to ensure success in negotiation.

2

Getting to win–win

In this chapter I look at the psychology behind negotiation, and how there are different approaches and styles depending on an individual's preferences and mindset when it comes to dealing with conflict.

Individual approaches to conflict

How do you approach a negotiation? Do you see it as a necessary evil, something to be dealt with quickly and pragmatically? Do you see it as a battle for supremacy, a competition where you need to push for as much as you can get and give away as little as possible? Do you see it as something which you would prefer to avoid doing, secretly hoping that the need might go away? Do you see it as something that you dislike as it highlights disagreement, so you are prepared to give in rather than risk damaging the relationship?

All of these different approaches are common reactions to conflict and reflect our own personal comfort zones, as well as our experience and learning about how to deal with these situations. None of them are truly satisfactory. Consider the following characters.

Sam

Sam is a corporate buyer. He plans and prepares well for negotiations with his suppliers, looking for their weak spots and choosing his tactics to exploit the power of his organisation. He enters the discussion by trying to overpower his suppliers by forcing them to accept his solution. He is aggressive at pursuing his own goals – to get the lowest possible price and the best possible deal for his company – at all costs, even if that means not being liked. He does not care if other people like or accept him: 'Business is business, it's not about friendships.'

Sam does not show his feelings or emotions, he sees them as signs of weakness, and ruthlessly exploits them when they appear on the other side of the table. Sam needs to win and to be seen to win. Winning gives him a sense of pride and achievement; losing gives him a sense of weakness and failure.

In other work relationships, Sam is the same. When any conflict occurs between people or departments, he is quick to battle for his side. If the other side doesn't fight back, it's their fault. 'It's a competitive environment – a dog eats dog world, so get your retaliation in first so as not to come out on the losing side.'

Terry

Terry works for the same company as Sam, in the accounting department, looking after accounts payable. She deals with a number of the supplier accounts that Sam has negotiated. Terry hates any form of conflict, and there are usually a lot of difficulties with Sam's accounts. The suppliers are always pestering her to get payment quickly. Terry believes this is because Sam has screwed the prices and conditions down so far in favour of the company that the suppliers are probably losing money on the contract. It takes up a lot of her time, and she hates answering the phone as there is usually an unhappy supplier at the other end of the line who dislikes the company. So Terry takes the line of least resistance and pays the invoices immediately, even though there are sometimes small errors in them. It's better to do this than have to address the issue – either with the supplier or (even more frighteningly) with Sam.

Terry tries to stay away from any issues where there might be conflict and from anyone who might think differently to her. It is hopeless to try to resolve conflicts, it just doesn't work. You come up against someone like Sam, and are worse off as a result. So it's easier to ignore conflict and hope it goes away.

Ted

Ted wants desperately to be accepted and liked by other people, both in and outside of work. He sees the way forward as trying to find every possible way to accommodate other people's requirements, even if that means putting himself out. So he finds himself often working late to get some detailed figures together which meets someone else's deadline. He finds it really difficult to say no, especially to buyers who are really challenging and pushy like Sam. Ted works for a company which is a key supplier to Sam's company, one of its biggest customers. He agreed to terms and a price that was not far above a break-even position for his company, at a time when it needed the business. Now he has to work really hard internally to make sure that his company can meet Sam's company's demands, which usually means Ted putting in the extra work to meet the requirements.

Ted could confront the issues, either with Sam or internally, but he is afraid of damaging the relationship which is vital to his company's survival. In any conflict someone gets hurt, so it is better to subjugate his and his company's needs in order to preserve the relationship.

Freda

Freda is buying a house. It is on the market for £200,000. However, she does not want to pay that much, she only wants to spend £160,000. The seller does not want to go that low, but does want to sell the house, so he offers to sell for £180,000. Freda agrees and the house is hers. The house is bought and sold, which was the main goal of both parties, but Freda paid £20,000 more than she wanted to and the seller sold for £20,000 less than he wanted.

Freda always walks the middle ground, seeking compromise and pragmatic solutions as quickly as possible to any problem or conflict issue that arises. She sees negotiation as a trade off – you give up something you want, the other party gives up something they want, and you get an agreement. OK, she is not wildly happy with the outcome a lot of the time, as she has had to compromise, but at least she has got something out of it, and something is better than nothing. It is impossible to get everything and be totally satisfied. Life is just a collection of compromises. You give up part of your goals and persuade the other party to give up part of theirs. There is usually a middle way where both parties can find some common ground and get something.

Winning and losing

In all of these scenarios there is an outcome which is not ideal.

Sam sees himself as winning his battles, but he is destroying trust and the relationships with those around him. His contracts look good at the time, but are not effective in the long run. His suppliers will probably reduce the quality or reliability in order to meet the strict terms of the price, with consequences for his company's own effectiveness. Sam's tactics allow him to win in the short term, but if he has to negotiate with the same person in the future, he will find the other party ready to seek revenge. Sam's initial win–lose approach ends up as lose–lose.

Terry and Ted put themselves on the losing side at the outset, and because they don't address the issues that confront them and their organisations, effective solutions will never be found. If it is impossible to raise areas of concern, then creative resolutions will never be developed. The issues fester and grow, and often boil over into aggressive or passive–aggressive responses where the attitude becomes one of 'I will not play with you' or 'I will take you down with me'. Again, a lose–lose outcome.

Freda uses compromise, which is a great tool for solving short-term disputes when the answer is to do some trading or haggling. It worked well in her house buying because neither she nor the seller needed to compromise on their goals, values or beliefs, they just needed to trade. But Freda finds it is not always enough to find a pragmatic solution without compromising on some of the goals, values or beliefs that she holds herself or are those of her organisation. She finds herself compromising anything and everything in the name of 'getting along' and for the sake of doing a deal. Some deal, any deal, is OK in this mindset. We are in the lose–lose arena again.

Can there ever be win–win?

If all of these scenarios end up in a lose–lose outcome in the long term, how do you get a win–win outcome. Surely if there is a winner, there has to be a loser? Consider Oliver's approach.

Example

Oliver is an ace negotiator with a major business. He is renowned for not only getting great deals for the organisation, but also building and maintaining long-term partnership relationships. He views all differences and conflicts as problems to be solved, and seeks a solution that achieves both his own goals and the goals of the other person. He sees the dialogue as an opportunity to improving the relationship with the other party by reducing tension and focusing on the conflict as a problem to be resolved.

Oliver puts in a lot of effort in preparation – he clearly thinks about what he and his organisation want, and more importantly does his homework on the other organisation. He tries his best to understand the dispute and the situation from the other side, empathising with their position. By looking clearly at both sides, and listening carefully

---

to what is said in the negotiation, he manages to find a solution that meets both their goals and resolves any tensions and negative feelings. By putting high value on the continuing relationship with the other party, he ensures that there is a willingness to collaborate and cooperate, and both parties see the longer-term benefits of a continuing relationship. Oliver has achieved a win–win result – both parties have achieved their goals in the negotiation and there is no underlying animosity or tension in the relationship that could impact on the deal or future negotiations.

One key difference here is Oliver's mindset. He believes that collaboration is the best approach to take. He does not see negotiation as a competitive activity, though he does stand up for his own needs and goals; and he does not see the outcome as either losing or winning. When confronted with conflict, he does not go into a defensive mode, he actively looks for opportunities to engage.

The different approaches to conflict are shown in Figure 2.1.

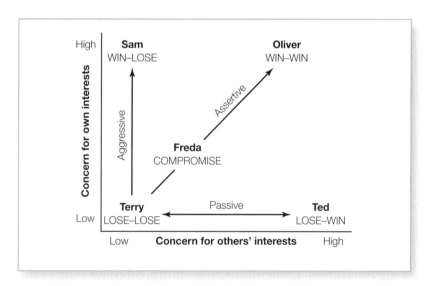

figure 2.1   Different approaches to conflict

Aggressive–assertive–passive continuum

Oliver's behaviour, described above, is not a natural behaviour pattern for most people when confronted by a stressor or aggressor. Our more natural response is often characterised by the fight–flight response, leading to aggressive–passive behaviour. Simply put, when an animal (including a human) is confronted by an aggressor, there are immediate physiological responses, such as the production of adrenaline, acceleration of heart and lung function and heightened arousal of the nervous system that allows the animal to engage in the intense muscular activity needed in order to stand and fight, or to run away (flight).

As humans, we very rarely confront lions or sabre toothed tigers on a daily basis, but our stress response is still triggered when we come into conflict with another, and feel threatened. Then our fight response manifests itself in aggressive, combative, argumentative behaviour and our flight is manifested through withdrawal, avoidance and self-deprecating behaviour. We have an aggressive–passive continuum of responses which make up our natural behaviour. We swing between these extremes like a pendulum, depending on the situation. Aggressive people follow a win–lose path, and passive people take a lose–win approach. When aggressive people meet other aggressive people, they fight until one wins and the other gives up (swings to passive mode). Passive people often swing to aggressive mode when pushed too far or too often (the cornered mouse syndrome). Neither is a healthy position for building relationships or for personal wellbeing.

Assertiveness is the middle point between the extremes of the continuum (See Figure 2.2). It is a learned rather than a natural behaviour, so it takes a conscious act to be assertive. Assertive communication strategies depend on approaches that protect the interests of both parties in the communication – yours and the other person's. You are able to effectively express your needs and concerns in a way that respects the needs and concerns of the other person. Both parties are able to conduct themselves in a way that expresses their needs and goals without forcing them on the other party (which would be aggressive) and in a climate where their needs and goals are valued (overcoming a passive response). Our natural responses are drawn to the middle of the continuum so that both parties can find a way forward that takes into account their own goals and needs. This allows for a win–win outcome.

Aggressive	Assertive	Passive
My needs paramount	Both needs important	My needs don't matter
Win–lose	Win–win	Lose–win

figure 2.2   Aggressive–assertive–passive continuum

The prisoners' dilemma

Sometimes lose–lose outcomes occur when win–win is possible. The classic example of this is called the prisoners' dilemma, a famous game theory exercise in which two prisoners must decide whether to confess to a crime. The classic situation is this: two people are arrested for a serious crime, but the police do not possess enough information to get a conviction. The police separate the two and offer both a similar deal – if one testifies against his partner and the other remains silent, the one who testifies goes free and the silent one receives the full sentence. If both remain silent, both are sentenced to only one month in jail for a minor charge. Each prisoner must choose either to betray or remain silent. What should they do?

In the game, the sole worry of the prisoners is to increase their own reward by lessening the time in jail. The best outcome for prisoner A is to confess, while prisoner B keeps quiet. In this case, prisoner A is rewarded by being set free, and the other (who stayed quiet) receives the maximum sentence. (This is a win–lose outcome – A wins, B loses.)

But the same logic applies for prisoner B. If B confesses and A remains silent, then B wins by being set free and A loses by getting the maximum sentence.

So, the logical decision leads each one to betray the other, even though their individual 'prize' would be greater if they both stayed silent. But as both prisoners confess (trying to take advantage of their partner), they each serve the maximum sentence (a lose–lose outcome). If neither confesses, they both serve a reduced sentence (a win–win outcome, although the win is not as big as the one they would have received in the win–lose scenario).

This game play may seem contrived, but there are in fact many examples in politics and business where the same outcomes occur. In international politics, for example, the prisoners' dilemma illustrates the problem of world trade. All parties reason that having free trade is beneficial, and all agree to remove trade barriers, but then immediately put on a tariff to protect one of their vital industries. The same is evident in discussions on global climate change. All countries will benefit from a stable climate, but any single country is often hesitant to curb CO_2 emissions. The immediate benefit to an individual country to maintain current behaviour is perceived to be greater than the eventual benefit to all countries if behaviour is changed, therefore explaining the current impasse.

In business, organisations continually play the prisoners' dilemma game by engaging in internal political battles and un-cooperative behaviour, thus making themselves less competitive in the external business environment. Others pursue policies that are designed to oust their competitors as opposed to maximising the performance of the firm. As the prisoners' dilemma shows win–win may not always appear to be the logical route, but collaboration usually has a better outcome.

Negotiation and win–win negotiation

A collaborative mindset and a viewpoint that goes beyond the quick win are the essential pre-conditions for a successful negotiation. In later chapters we will investigate some of the complexities in the process and identify ways of ensuring that negotiations are even more successful. To start with, it helps to have some definitions.

Negotiation

Negotiation has been part of social interaction for centuries, going right back to the fairly primitive agreements forged between individuals and hunter-gatherer bands to form the early communities and societies. The common structure for traditional negotiation, detailed by Gavin Kennedy, is: 'two parties meeting as principals or through representatives, exchanging their different solutions to the common problem both parties faced, until a common solution acceptable to both parties was reached or the parties broke off in frustration or discord'.[1]

Over the years, the 'win at any costs' lobby has developed tricks and ploys to gain advantage by being 'street smart', whilst the collaborative lobby has moved to devise principles to change the adversarial approach into a more 'principled' approach that leads to longer-term

---

[1] Kennedy, Gavin (2009) *Essential Negotiation: An A–Z Guide*, London, The Economist/Profile Books Ltd., p. 2.

and more lasting agreements. The flaw with the street smart approach is that for every ploy there is an antidote – and even if you are successful, it leads to retaliatory actions and loss of respect when the other party finds out it has been tricked. This book will look at a number of the ploys and tricks, as it is likely that some will be used even in the most principled approach, but the overwhelming emphasis will be on negotiation strategies and tactics that lead to long-term, successful, win–win outcomes.

Win–win negotiation

Taking into account the essential characteristics of a successful outcome, a working definition for win–win negotiation is as follows:

> *Win–win negotiation is an interactive process where two or more parties with common and conflicting interests come together to exchange ideas and propositions in order to reach an agreement where they all leave with a desirable result, after fully taking into account each others' interests.*

Some specific parts of this definition are worthy of more emphasis:

■ *Interactive*: negotiation involves dialogue and interaction. This may be face-to-face or conducted through technology, but it involves exchange. This differentiates negotiation from 'take it or leave it' which involves no interaction.

■ *Process*: negotiation is a process with a start and an end, and it is the means to get to the desired end. It involves the journey to the destination not the destination itself. This doesn't mean losing sight of the destination, but rather paying more attention to how we get there.

■ *Two or more parties*: negotiation involves at least two different parties, who may be individuals, departments, organisations or nations.

■ *Common and conflicting interests*: if there is no common interest, then the parties will not be able to engage with each other. If there is no conflicting interest, there is no dispute. In order to negotiate there must be both (though in many cases the commonality and/or difference may not be immediately obvious and needs to be clarified before substantive dialogue can take place).

■ *Come together to exchange ideas and propositions*: negotiation is two way; it assumes that both parties are willing to engage with each other (albeit through a mediator or third party in some cases of deep seated or acrimonious conflict).

▓ *In order to reach an agreement*: negotiation is not a game; it has an end goal and that end goal is to reach an agreement. If either party has no intention of reaching an agreement, then you cannot negotiate.

▓ *All leave with a desirable result, after fully taking into account each others' interests*: this is what makes a negotiation into a win–win negotiation. The parties concerned **all** leave with a **desirable result**. They can only do this by fully understanding and taking into account the others' interests.

In the next chapter I explore the negotiation process that will enable you to achieve win–win outcomes. In the meantime, you might like to reflect on your own preferred negotiation style – do you behave more like Sam, Terry, Ted, Freda or Oliver? Do you approach a conflict situation from the mindset of competing, avoiding, accommodating, compromising or collaborating? Do you have a view that if there is a winner then there has to be a loser, or can you see how both parties can 'win'?

3

The negotiation process

Win–win negotiation is an interactive process where two or more parties with common and conflicting interests come together to exchange ideas and propositions in order to reach an agreement where they all leave with a desirable result, after fully taking into account each others' interests.

This was the definition I introduced at the end of the last chapter, and describes the integral parts of a successful negotiation. In this chapter, I detail the interactive process that all negotiations follow through a number of phases. In common with any other process, the failure to complete a phase successfully, or to miss a phase altogether, will compromise the outcome. The phases are not necessarily a linear progression – you can return to a phase if something new crops up during discussion – but each phase needs to be completed successfully for an optimal outcome.

The three phases of a negotiation

There are three major phases to a negotiation: preparation, interaction and implementation, with the interaction phase being further subdivided into four further phases (see Figure 3.1).

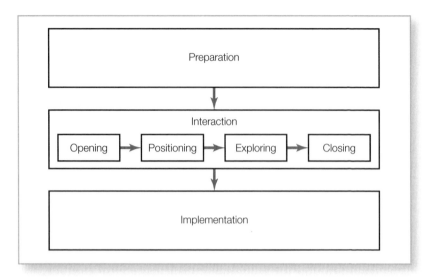

figure 3.1   **Phases of a negotiation**

The preparation phase

The clear and unequivocal starting point for any negotiation is preparation. There is an old adage: 'If you fail to prepare, then prepare to fail.' In negotiating this is particularly true. The research evidence is clear: successful negotiators spend more time planning than average negotiators, and spend more time considering the negotiation from the other party's perspective rather than their own.

Preparing for a negotiation is not just reading up on the situation – it is knowing your business, understanding your motivations, knowing your skills, developing strategies and tactics, considering physical and emotional issues that might arise, knowing your limits, knowing your stakeholders' needs, knowing what is important and not important (and being able to differentiate between importance and urgency) – in short, knowing as much as it is possible to know before venturing into the negotiating arena. And the most important preparation is knowing all of these things, and more, about your opposite party in the negotiation; which means doing research in all of those areas where you have no immediate information, so that when the negotiation starts, you are in the best possible position.

Research evidence from successful negotiators finds that they spend more time than average negotiators in the preparation phase, and more of that time thinking and preparing from the other party's viewpoint.

Preparation is one of those areas where time is well spent, but there is no direct correlation between time spent and successful outcomes. Just because you spend longer preparing doesn't mean you will be more successful. But not spending enough time will seriously limit your ability to succeed. Preparation time needs to be limited to the amount that is relevant to the situation. You would not want to spend several days researching and preparing for a negotiation on a trivial matter; but you certainly do not want to go into a major business or life negotiation after just a few minutes' thinking time.

Use the following questions to help you to decide how long and how much effort to put in.

A 12-point preparation phase checklist

1 What is the situation?

Each negotiation is different, regardless of whether you have negotiated with the person before or have encountered similar situations. Always start out afresh and think through from the beginning. It may help you to avoid the trap of making an assumption that is not valid. Consider the following questions:

- Have you been here before? What was the result?
- Have you negotiated with this person/organisation before? What was the result?
- How well do you know the other party?
- What is the history of the relationship?
- How important is this relationship to you? To your organisation? To the other party? To the other party's organisation?
- Is the issue clearly defined?
- Is the issue accepted and understood by both parties?
- How important is resolving this issue to you? To your organisation? To the other party? To the other party's organisation?
- How urgent is resolving this issue to you? To your organisation? To the other party? To the other party's organisation?

2 What is the scope?

Is the issue a 'one-off' or is it part of a continuing or potential longer-term relationship? You will want to spend more time and effort if this negotiation is in the latter category, unless the one-off deal is very large and important.

3 What type of conflict is underlying?

In Chapter 1, we identified two major groupings of conflict: objective (the source is more tangible and measurable, like resources) and psychological (the source is more subjective and personal). On which side does this conflict lie, or is it a combination of both? How does the other party view it?

By analysing the type of conflict, you achieve a better understanding of the real depth of the conflict, and the potential ease or difficulty faced in resolving it. In the main, objective conflicts are generally easier to specify and resolve. Psychological conflicts are more difficult to address and resolve as perceptions and opinions play a larger part. Mixed conflicts, where both objective and psychological causes are present, are the most difficult, as one party may see the situation very differently to the other.

4 Does this affect anything else?

Will this negotiation affect other negotiations or agreements? Are there any international interests? It is vital that you consider the impact or consequences of a negotiation in the preparation phase in order to assess what you need to take into account in the planning phase.

5 Do you need to negotiate?

Is there an alternative strategy to negotiating that could be successful? There are different strategies for resolving conflict as identified in Chapter 1. At this stage it is worth considering whether you have to negotiate. What would be the impact of not negotiating? What else could you do? The less options, the more important it is to prepare for a successful negotiation.

6 Who is involved?

Who are the stakeholders in this negotiation? Where do they sit in terms of relationship and agreement with the goal? Do you need prior agreement before embarking on the negotiation? Will your agreement require formal approval? Who is involved on the other side of the negotiation?

Generally speaking, the more stakeholders that are involved and the more formal the agreement process, the greater the need for preparation.

7 How urgent are matters?

What are the deadlines on both sides? Is the clock already ticking? How much time do you have available?

8 Where will you negotiate?

Are you playing at home or away? Just like a sports team, there are different strategies to apply if you have a home advantage or if you are playing away.

Do you have influence over the location? Is this something you want to negotiate? For sensitive negotiations, like labour disputes, a neutral location might be the preferred choice so that no-one has the psychological and resource advantage. If the negotiation is particularly sensitive, it may be necessary to make the location a subject for an initial negotiation (e.g. as in the case of international disputes).

How far away from support will you be? The further away, the more preparation is needed. For international negotiations, it is not easy to pop back to the office to check some details, so you need to make sure you have everything prepared and with you. You also need to be psychologically prepared to be at a distance from support and in a different culture. Poor preparation here can be costly both in a poor outcome and in air fares!

9 Are you in the public eye?

The greater the importance and interest in the negotiation, the more you will be in the spotlight, internally and possibly externally. And therefore the more you will want to prepare.

What is the spotlight like from the other side? In international negotiations, what seems like a trivial matter to one side can be of extreme public interest to the other. (When I was doing some consultancy work in South-West Russia in the early days following the break up of the USSR, a simple local negotiation on providing development workshops for local businessmen in Rostov-on-Don was – without my prior knowledge or any warning – subject to major publicity by the local TV news, with live interviews conducted as we walked out of the discussion.)

10 Any other third parties involved?

Are there any agents, intermediaries, translators, consultants, specialists or officials who will be involved, from either side. Will there be a neutral third party facilitator or chairperson? If so, you will need to prepare more with their roles in mind.

11 Who makes the decisions?

Do you have authority to agree on behalf of your organisation? Does the other party have authority to agree on behalf of their organisation? Do you need to negotiate internally in order to identify your authority level? Do you need to make this an issue in the negotiation with the other party so that the right person is in the room?

12 Who can help you?

'A problem shared is a problem halved.'

This is true for preparing for a negotiation as much as in other areas of life. A second pair of eyes is always helpful when considering all of the different perspectives and interests involved in conflict and negotiation situations. This helps us to challenge our assumptions and to look from the other side of the fence. Talking through the situation, or planning, with someone else has real benefits, even in seemingly simple situations.

Asking yourself these 12 questions will help you to determine how much effort and how much time you should devote to the preparation phase. There is a lot of other detailed planning and preparation to carry out so that you enter the negotiation itself in the best position to guarantee success. How do you start? What are you going to offer? What is your back-up plan? What questions will you ask? What do you really need? What does the other party want? How will your personality help or hinder? What form of agreement is needed? How will you address difficulties that you might encounter?

These, and many more detailed planning questions relate to how you are going to plan for and manage the actual negotiation itself. This is the interaction phase, and although you cannot predict everything that will happen when dialogue actually starts, you can do a lot of preparatory work that will mean there are fewer surprises when you do start talking. Chapter 5 is devoted to the detailed elements and questions involved in the preparation of the interaction phase, which is the next phase in the negotiation process.

The interaction phase

This is the phase involving the negotiation arena – whether negotiation is conducted face-to-face or remotely; whether it is conducted one-to-one or in teams; whether it is formal or informal, whether it is a one-off meeting or spread over days, months or years. This phase is a process in its own right, and one that can be planned for and managed. Successful management of the interaction phase will mean that you have a greater chance of getting to a win–win outcome, even if the other party does not enter the arena with the same intention.

The OPEC model

OPEC is the acronym formed from the initial letters of the four phases of interaction: opening, positioning, exploring and closing (see Figure 3.2).[2] Each phase of the OPEC model has two actions that need to be completed in order to achieve its objective (see Figure 3.3). The best results come from completing one phase successfully before moving to the next phase; however that does not prevent moving back to a previous phase if difficulties emerge later in the process. What is important is that all of the actions and phases are completed satisfactorily.

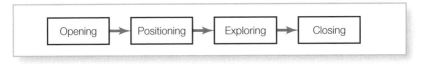

figure 3.2   The OPEC model

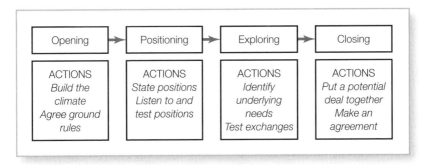

figure 3.3   The OPEC phases and actions

[2] It is also the acronym of the Organisation of Petroleum Exporting Countries who, being a cartel, are not necessarily a good role model for negotiating practice. However, participants on my negotiation courses who come from OPEC member countries, or the oil industry in general, appreciate the link!

Opening

In the opening phase, the intention is to create a positive climate where the two parties can confirm their intention to cooperate and collaborate together, not just for the duration of the interaction phase, but also for the implementation phase. The focus is on building the relationship, establishing a common ground and agreeing the ground rules necessary to ensure there is effective interaction and grounds for a mutually acceptable and implementable agreement.

Objective
To create a positive atmosphere and success goal for the negotiation

Action step: build the climate
Take action to build a positive climate for the negotiation. This includes seating arrangements, welcoming the other party, making introductions, establishing rapport, building a collaborative atmosphere, expressing expectations, expressing the desire to engage and seek a positive resolution, listening to the other party's expectations, surfacing all concerns, and ensuring all are comfortable before moving to the next action.

Action step: agree ground rules
Set out and agree an agenda and timetable for the negotiation, identifying expectations from both sides, clarifying any procedural issues or protocols, agreeing the format for the final agreement or any stages that need to be addressed, establishing authority to agree, and agreeing any interaction guidelines to manage the dialogue.

Positioning

In the positioning phase, the focus is on stating – and testing – each other's starting point or position on the issue, initially to see whether there is an easy solution that can be derived from the data and reasoning already to hand, or whether the gap between the two parties' positions is such that you need to move further in the negotiation process. If the parties need to move further from their opening positions then they need to stop trying to persuade each other by offering more and more arguments and suggestions to solve the problem – as it is now clear it cannot be solved through logical persuasion and argument.

Objective
To identify the opening positions of both parties and the gap between these positions.

Action step: state positions
Each party states its opening positions. What does each see as the key elements of the negotiation, what does each want to achieve in the negotiation, what does each see as its initial offer to resolve the issue.

Action step: listen to and test positions
Ask questions and summarise what has been heard to check understanding of the other party's opening position statements. Ask probing questions to test the strength of the position of the other party, and the degree of willingness to move from that position and consider other alternatives. Clearly state one's strength of position and degree of willingness to move from that position and consider other alternatives.

Exploring

In the exploring phase the focus is on probing and identifying the other party's underlying needs for the negotiation; to understand what they really want, what their real interests are. As the parties probe and understand what is driving their position, then they can try to find alternative ways of satisfying these needs that were not immediately obvious in the preparation or positioning phase. The parties also need to disclose their own needs and interests. Not only does this build trust and relationship by showing openness and the willingness to take a risk, but it will also allow more possibilities to emerge for exchanges with the other party that will satisfy your needs and were not predicted. This is the power of the exploring phase – being able to uncover opportunities for exchanges to be tested to see whether they meet the underlying needs of the two parties, many of which did not emerge in the preparation phase.

Many negotiations fail because they do not transfer effectively from the positioning phase to the exploring phase. The parties fail to reach agreement as they keep trying to persuade the other party that their ideas for a solution are the best – and the other party is doing the same. They get into a deadlock situation where compromise (agreeing to something just for the sake of reaching an outcome) or failure are the only possible outcomes.

Both in preparation and the negotiating arena parties confuse what they **want** (our position) with what they **need**. A simple example: I wake up in the middle of the night and I need a sandwich. I go down to the kitchen to discover there is no bread, no butter, no cheese, no ham. I therefore go back to bed unsatisfied as I can't get what I need.

However, if I recognised that my real need is to satisfy my hunger, then I might notice some alternatives in the kitchen, like some fruit. I will only find the possible alternatives if I understand that a sandwich is just something I want, and is just one way of satisfying my underlying need. It is a solution I have come up with, but by no means the only possible solution. In negotiation, as in satisfying my night-time hunger, understanding my needs and the other party's needs are critical to finding win–win outcomes.

Objective
To discover the underlying needs of the parties and identify potential alternative exchanges that could meet these needs.

Action step: identify underlying needs
Ask questions to probe the drivers behind the other party's position. Listen and summarise to check understanding of the other party's needs. Ask questions to identify what is important to the other party and what is less important. Disclose your underlying needs to the other party and what is more and less important.

Action step: test exchanges
From an understanding of the other party's needs, suggest possible offers that might be of interest. Ask the other party to consider offers made to you that would satisfy your needs. Seek creative exchanges of low cost and high value. Test possible exchanges, 'If I did this and you did that, would that work?'

Closing

Once the options and possibilities uncovered in the exploring phase have been uncovered, it is possible to finally put together a deal in the closing stage, assemble the package and make an agreement that now satisfies both parties. The form of closure will differ with the type of negotiation. Some will have detailed, written agreements; some will be in the form of contracts and legal documents; many others will be an informal understanding – the equivalent of a handshake. Whatever the form of the agreement, what is important is that it is clear and understood by both parties, otherwise there will be difficulties in the implementation phase of the negotiation.

Objective
To put together a final agreement.

Action step: put a potential deal together
Develop a potential package of exchanges that have been raised during
the exploring phase that might resolve the issue. Listen to any potential
package of exchanges that the other party sees would resolve the issue.
Work together to refine the package so that both parties are satisfied.

Action step: make an agreement
Summarise the final details of the agreed package. Put together an
agreement in the format required by the two parties (ideally agreed in
the ground rules action step) – formal, written, legal, informal, verbal,
handshake, signed, referred for approval, etc. Celebrate success.

The Implementation phase

My first job as a graduate management trainee was as a sales representative in South Wales where I learned a fundamental lesson – that
the sale is not completed until the invoice has been paid. The same
is true for a negotiation – the negotiation is not complete until the
agreement has been implemented. The best negotiations try to predict
and overcome potential problems and pitfalls in the implementation
phase, but they are unlikely to cover every eventuality. So this phase
is equally important – though often neglected by the buyer or seller
in their rush to get an agreement. This phase is even more important
where the people responsible for the implementation are not the
same as the people who conducted the initial negotiation. In these
situations implementation issues arise because those assigned with
implementation do not have a shared history or understanding of the
terms of the agreement.

Effective agreements anticipate the future. They address what happens if there are disagreements during implementation and how to
monitor the performance of the agreement. In simple situations, this
just means identifying and confirming that the delivery of goods has
been received on time, to the quality specified and at the right price.
In a more complex, longer-term agreement – like partnerships – there
needs to be a much more detailed agreement of communication and
monitoring of frequency and processes, and agreed conditions that
would trigger renegotiation and changes to the agreement.

You may also need to spell out actions that would be taken to deal
with any violation of the terms of the agreement, what should happen
if a party feels its interests are being threatened because expected
results do not come about or unanticipated consequences result, and

even for termination of the agreement. In one agreement for partnership working with colleagues in the consulting industry, we put more emphasis in the agreement on how to leave the partnership rather than putting in clauses that kept the partnership together. This recognised the fact that the partnership would not function properly if one of the parties wanted to leave, so rather than forcing agreements to stay connected, we made how to leave clear and transparent.

In longer-term agreements, creating opportunities for bringing the parties together to review the agreement or parts of the agreement makes good sense. And it makes good sense that the parties who initiated the agreement should also be involved in these reviews, even if the implementation has transferred to other parties in the respective organisations. Good purchasing agreements in companies allow for regular communication in this way between the buyer and seller representatives and the operational management responsible for the execution of the contract.

Even if the agreement is going well, it is a good idea to communicate between both parties on a regular basis to exchange information, celebrate success and address any new issues that might arise. At the heart of win–win negotiation is a desire to collaborate and cooperate, so time spent in maintaining a good relationship is well spent in nurturing this collaboration and to provide a platform for further collaboration in the future. Collaboration means a commitment to meeting the needs of all the parties, so continued communication is a must.

There is no fixed formula or process for implementation, as every agreement is unique. But to ignore it in the euphoria of getting the initial signature is tempting fate, and fate in these situations nearly always comes up with further problems and issues. Just like in the preparation phase, the amount of time and effort needed in the implementation phase will change according to the importance and complexity of the negotiation and the short- or long-term nature of the agreement. The following questions will help to define the amount of effort that should be considered:

A 12-point implementation phase checklist

1 What is the situation?

What is the overall situation regarding this negotiation and the agreement? If the situation is new, then there may be more implementation issues. If this is an agreement with a known party on a regular subject, there are less likely to be implementation issues, or the issues may be easier to predict.

■ What has been the history with this party? Good or bad? New or established? Positive or difficult?

■ Is this a new agreement with a known party? A new agreement with a new party?

■ How important is this agreement to you? To your organisation? To the other party? To the other party's organisation?

■ What is the time frame of the agreement?

2 What is the scope?

■ Is the agreement a 'one-off supply'? Part of a continuing, or potential longer-term relationship? A partnership?

■ Is the implementation simple or complex?

Longer-term partnership agreements will require greater effort in the implementation phase.

3 What was the experience of the negotiation?

A negotiation that was carried out easily and successfully with goodwill and relationship building on both sides is likely to have less implementation issues – and those that do occur will probably be easier to resolve due to the relationship and communication history of the two parties.

4 Does this agreement affect others?

If there is an impact or consequence of an agreement on other agreements or operations, then there are some complex relationships at work which could mean more frequent and more difficult implementation issues.

5 Are the initial negotiators involved in implementation?

If the original negotiators are not involved in the implementation, then the history and detailed background of the agreement is not easily to hand, so implementation issues are more likely to arise as the operators try to interpret the terms and conditions of the agreement.

6 Who else is involved?

The more people involved in implementation, the greater the likelihood of issues arising. Every divergence from a standard will increase the possibility of a different interpretation and cause an implementation issue. Consider the supply of raw materials in differing

quantities, to different locations in different countries, in different
languages and currencies, in metric or imperial weights, with different quality acceptance standards, with different purchasing and
payment arrangements . . .

7 How important is the agreement?

How significant is the agreement to the operational integrity of each
of the parties? For example, if it is the supply of a vital raw material to
a production process that carries little, if any, buffer stock, then the
implementation of the supply agreement needs to be very carefully
and closely monitored to ensure continuity of production. This is
incredibly important to the producing company, but the supplier may
not see or feel the same level of importance and give the right level of
urgency to any glitch in the supply chain.

The degree of importance of the agreement suggests the amount of
attention that should be paid to anticipating implementation issues
and providing mechanisms for their speedy resolution.

8 How important is a continuing relationship?

You may see the agreement as an end in itself or the opportunity to
build or maintain an on-going relationship with the other party. If
you favour the latter, then you will want to put more effort into implementation in order to cement the bonds and keep the communication
and relationship channels open.

9 How far away is the action?

In internationally significant deals, the agreement may be implemented in a different country, region or continent with different time
zones, languages and cultures. This makes monitoring more difficult.
Some cultures see negotiation and agreement differently – in Western
countries agreements and contracts are viewed as fixed and binding, in
some other countries there is a culture of greater flexibility. Contracts
and agreements are seen as guidelines that can be renegotiated as operational issues arise. This difference of interpretation can lead to serious
implementation issues, especially when the contracts and agreements
are being administered at a distance.

10 Who has the authority?

Where does authority to make interpretations of the agreement lie?
On your side? On the other party's side?

The more levels that are involved in making interpretations and adjustments to the operational implementation of the agreement, the more complex and difficult the implementation process.

11 What can go wrong?

After considering all of the implementation pitfalls and possibilities, it is always worthwhile thinking again about what might go wrong. At the end of any negotiation, the success of the agreement often blinds us to some factors that we, or the other party, have missed. Consideration of what might go wrong early in the implementation phase will help to identify issues before they grow to a point where they can derail the whole agreement and relationship. Conducting a risk analysis may be useful.

12 What else can go wrong?

And after conducting a risk analysis and considering all angles for the implementation of the agreement, think again!

The next chapter, which concludes Part 1, examines the communication skills necessary in a negotiation. These are particularly relevant and important during the interaction phase when you are in dialogue with the other party.

4

Communication styles essential to negotiating

If preparation is one of the keys to ensuring success in a negotiation, then another, equally important key is the ability to communicate effectively, not just to understand and influence the other party in the negotiation, but also to communicate effectively with all of the other stakeholders who have an interest in the outcome of the negotiation. In this chapter, I outline the communication styles that are essential to the successful completion of the interaction phase of a negotiation. These styles are described in more detail in my book *Getting Results Without Authority: The new rules of organisational influence*[1] where I explore the process of influencing in organisations.

The definition of win–win negotiation I introduced in Chapter 2 – 'an interactive process where two or more parties with common and conflicting interests come together to exchange ideas and propositions in order to reach an agreement where they all leave with a desirable result, after fully taking into account each others' interests' – confirms the importance of communication in a negotiation. Some negotiations may take place remotely and via technology where there is no face-to-face interaction and sometimes no real time communication, but there is still interaction and communication – and it could be argued that these remote environments are fraught with more communication difficulties, so require greater skill and ability.

---

[1] Cox, Geof (2010) *Getting Results Without Authority: The new rules of organisational influence*, www.BookShaker.com.

The four styles of communication

If you observe how people interact with you and with each other, you will notice different styles of communication. Some people are very direct, to the point and positive in asserting their wishes and requirements. They let others know what is wanted from them and are quick to tell others when they are pleased or dissatisfied. They use their authority to get others to do what is wanted, getting people to agree with plans and proposals and then follow up to make sure people carry out their agreements. They have a strength in bargaining, doing deals with others all the time to get things done.

Other people follow a more measured and systematic approach. They produce detailed and comprehensive proposals for dealing with problems, presenting the logic behind ideas and using facts, arguments and opinions to support their position. They are quick to grasp the strengths and weaknesses in an argument and to see and articulate the logical connections between different aspects of a complex situation. They are unemotional and follow a very logical and rational approach in their communication.

Then there are the people who openly and readily admit to not having all of the answers. They will spend time and listen attentively to the ideas and feelings of others, actively showing interest in others' contributions and trying to understand different points of view. They are willing to be influenced by others whilst also pursuing their own objectives. They appreciate and support others' ideas and accomplishments and they make sure everyone is heard before a decision is made. This group of people are renowned for building powerful and strong relationships by showing trust in others and helping to bring out the best in them.

Finally, you will see the group of people who appeal to the emotions and ideals of others through the use of forceful and colourful words and images. They demonstrate an enthusiasm for the future which is contagious. They bring people together by articulating a vision of future possibilities. They see the exciting potential in an idea or situation and can communicate that excitement to others. They are adept at getting others to see the values, hopes and aspirations which they have in common and build these common values into a shared sense of loyalty and commitment.

That is not to say that people only use one of these communication styles. Most of us use a mix of these styles, though we tend to have a preference for using one or two of them more than the others. These are styles that we find easy to use; styles that get us results most of the time; styles that we have been taught to use through school and training; styles that fit the cultures we live and work in; and styles that fit our values and beliefs.

So someone who has learned to think and act in a logical and rational way and is working in an organisation that is practical and systematic in its approach is likely to use a rational approach to communication, basing their interactions on facts, rules, procedures and logical argument. By contrast, someone who has learned to value and care about people and works in an organisation that is based on team work, self-development and respect for the worth of the individual is likely to use a more people oriented approach, interacting more with feelings and emotions and seeking to understand.

If someone has strong tendencies in these directions, they will find it difficult to communicate effectively with someone from an opposite preference and therefore influence them. On the other hand, they will work effectively with people who share their mindset. In a tight, line management structure, different groups may exhibit similar characteristics – they have similar cultures and will have recruited people with traits that tend to fit. However, modern organisations and matrix/project structures encourage more cross-functional dialogue and the opportunity for different preferences and cultures to clash. So the more we can develop flexibility and adapt our style to meet the preference of the other party, the greater will be our capacity to communicate effectively and exert influence.

In the negotiation arena, as we will see later in this chapter, the effective use of all four communication styles is essential in order to successfully complete a negotiation. So negotiators need to build the competence and confidence to use all the styles and to become adept at moving between them flexibly.

There are two main dimensions of behaviour in communication: the degree to which we are directive, and the degree to which we are responsive. People who are directive tend to be seen as more forceful and assertive, taking control, making quick decisions and taking more risks. People who are responsive will be sensitive to, and willing to share, emotions and feelings, appear more friendly and are concerned about relationships. There are no absolutes in these two dimensions, as we are all directive and responsive to some extent, but we all have preferences. Our influence patterns can thus be broken down into four styles (see Figure 4.1).

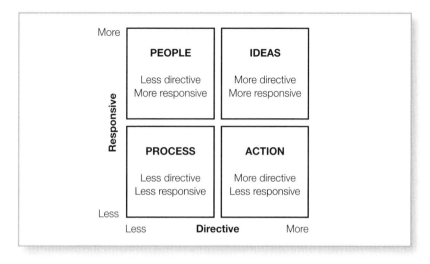

figure 4.1   **The four communication styles**

A note on the names of the four communication styles. I am using words in the style names to describe a way of communicating. Do not take the names too literally. For instance, using the word 'idea' in conversation does not mean the person is using the ideas style. You can present an 'idea' in any of the four styles. Similarly, a low preference for the people style does not mean you dislike people, just that you use the people style less. This is particularly important for readers whose first language is not English; literal translation of the words may infer a different meaning.

Developing your communication style

Knowing your own preferred style and that of others helps you to know your strengths and areas for development. Take notice of how you communicate with others and how they communicate with you. What style do they typically use? What style do you typically use? What style do others use? Which styles have a positive impact on you? Which style do you find more challenging when others use them? Which styles do you find easy? Which styles do you find difficult?

In a negotiation each of the styles is needed, so we need to develop flexibility to use each style, and also to respond positively to each one. We need to identify those areas where working in partnership with other people in a negotiation team, where the strengths and weaknesses of each member complement the others, would be particularly beneficial.

The four communication styles, their behaviours and outcomes are summarised in Figure 4.2 and discussed in detail below.

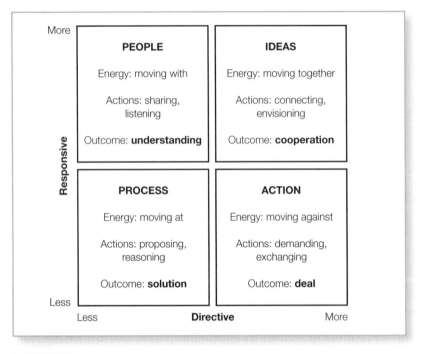

figure 4.2   The four communication styles, their behaviours and outcomes

Action style

Description	People talk about:	People are:
The action-oriented mindset is fundamentally geared to changing things, improving existing situations, translating ideas into actions, being effective, getting things done, moving ahead and achieving good results. Preferred type of agreement: *deal*. Preferred style of discourse: *bargaining*.	Results Objectives Performance Deals Challenges Moving ahead Responsibility Achievements Change Decisions	Pragmatic Direct Impatient Decisive Quick Energetic Challenging

Action people are task-oriented, keen to get things done, decisive and direct (more directive and less responsive). They use an energy that is *moving against* others, and can therefore be seen as forceful, pushy and aggressive if they overuse or misuse the approach.

Underuse of this style means that you will not be able to get things done quickly and may miss deadlines. The people you negotiate with may not have the clarity about what precisely you want from them and by when. So agreements will not be clear and may be open to misinterpretation. Overusing the style, or not using both of the actions, can be perceived as arrogant, aggressive and dictatorial – you are only interested in getting what you want and not giving anything in return.

Effective use of the style comes from balancing the two behaviours – demanding and exchanging. The outcome is a **deal**:

> *'If you agree to do X for me, I will do Y for you.'*
> *'In return for the car, I will give you the money.'*

Action style depends on the exchange you can make to influence someone to do something for you. The exchange can be obvious and material, based on the resources, position or information you have: a tip, promotion, contract, salary increase, gifts, information that the other party needs. Exchanges can also be less obvious and not material, based more on personal power: approval, status, attention, praise, inclusion, time. These latter, psychological exchanges are often more powerful and longer lasting than material ones.

The exchange backs up the demand that we are making. It has to be something that the giver has to offer, something that the receiver desires and considers of sufficient value to balance the demand made. The critical point for the influencer is that it is the perception of value and balance in the eyes of the receiver which is important, not the giver's idea of what is appropriate. Thus something of low cost to the giver, like praise, can be viewed as of immense value by the receiver.

In a negotiation, you need to pull together the elements of the agreement that have been discussed and make a clear statement of the exchanges and demands from both sides that make the deal. You may also need to make consequences very clear during the negotiation when the action style could be usefully applied.

Process style

Description	People talk about:	People are:
The process-oriented mindset is characterised by the need to know, be factual, understand, organise, structure, set up strategies, tactics, establish rules, regulations, systems and manage. Preferred type of agreement: *logical solution*. Preferred style of discourse: debate.	Facts Details Observations Procedures Planning Proof Organising Controlling Testing Analysis	Systematic Logical Factual Verbose Unemotional Cautious Patient

Process-style people also use a pushing type of energy, but are less directive and forceful, relying more on the logical and rational nature of their argument, *moving at* the other party in order to reach a solution. Overuse or misuse of this style results in inflexible sets of rules and procedures, bureaucracy and verbosity. It is a favourite style of communication for many people and for business, especially as the first resort.

The process style uses logical reasoning and debate in order to create structure in data and facts, and by analysis finds the best solution to the problem or situation being faced. It is an essential style in a negotiation to set out the facts and details involved from both sides, and to put together potential propositions for logically solving the issue.

Overuse or an imbalance of the two actions in this style can lead to bureaucracy, long and boring meetings, and slavish following of procedures and rules – even when it is clear that the procedure is not effective. That makes negotiations tiresome for both sides. It is a favourite style of many organisations as it allows some degree of participation in decision making but it is not an appropriate style to use if a quick decision is needed or where you are not open to other options.

Effective use of the style comes from balancing the two behaviours – proposing and reasoning. The outcome is a **solution**:

> *'The conclusion from the analysis of the data suggests that we take this course of action.'*

'Weighing up the arguments on both sides, there is nothing to be gained from taking immediate action as the decision deadline is not until the end of the financial year, and there is no penalty for delaying the decision. Delaying the decision and gathering more data seems to be the best solution.'

The reasoning backing up the proposal needs to be valid and based on facts and logic. It is the weight of argument which influences, not in quantity but in quality. Reasoning that is geared towards the receiver, not the influencer, has the most impact. A strong reason for doing something from one perspective may hold no weight for the other person. So thinking in terms of benefits and what is important to the receiver is vital for success.

Quantity of argument is attractive, but ineffective. It is often perceived as trying to wear down the other party into submission through the sheer weight of data and argument. It also tends toward the verbose, so you need to control the urge to continue talking or writing so that you don't find yourself snatching defeat from the jaws of victory by having to defend a poorly researched piece of data or rationale which was not necessary. With proper preparation, a good proposal should not need more than two or three reasons to back it up. As a colleague and mentor, Walt Hopkins, puts it:

'Propose precisely, reason concisely, then shut up nicely.'

People style

Description	People talk about:	People are:
The people-oriented mindset is characterised by men and women who care about people, have a strong drive towards people's needs, rights, communication, understanding each other, team work, ethics, synergy, feelings and emotions. Preferred type of agreement: *empathy*. Preferred style of discourse: *understanding*.	People Needs Self-development Sensitivity Relationships Motivations Beliefs Values Awareness Cooperation Communications Feelings Team spirit Understanding	Spontaneous Empathetic Warm Subjective Emotional Perceptive Sensitive

The people style uses listening and sharing to help people to build understanding. The energy used is *moving with*, using the energy of the other person in a positive way to develop a relationship, not to manipulate or dominate. The mindset of people orientation is characterised by a strong desire towards teamwork, synergy, communication and the needs of others. It is empathetic and sensitive.

People style is the only style that gathers information, so it is very useful to help find out what values and desires the other party has which can then be used as possible exchanges, reasons or connections. It therefore has a strong strategic use. It also builds relationships with others through developing deeper understanding of each other. It is therefore a key style to use where relationship and trust are critical.

This style does take up more time than any of the other styles, both to build rapport and to listen effectively. But if deeper insight into the thinking of the other person is important, then it is time and effort that is well spent.

Effective use of the people style, as with all of the other styles, comes from balancing the two behaviours – sharing and listening. The outcome is **understanding**:

> *'I am confused by the aims of this project and I need your help to understand what I need to focus on (sharing)... If I hear you correctly, your priority is that we must keep to the time deadlines at all cost. Could you expand on the importance of keeping to time so I can understand why it is more important than keeping to the specification (listening)?'*

Sharing allows you to open up to the other party and show that you are willing to disclose information and feelings. This builds trust and gives the other party the confidence to reciprocate. Sharing too much will tend to have the opposite effect and erode trust as people will feel 'dumped' upon. Listening too much, or listening selectively, will also build mistrust and the feeling of being manipulated, so it is important to balance sharing with listening.

Empathetic listening is listening with the intent to understand. It is the highest level of listening, the others being:

- ignoring: staying quiet but not paying any attention to what the person is saying;
- pretending: using verbal or non-verbal clues but not really listening;
- selective: hearing only certain parts of what the person is saying – usually those parts we agree with;
- attentive: actively paying attention and focusing on understanding what is being said.

Empathetic listening is listening to really understand the other person's frame of reference – to see and feel the world as they do.[2]

Tips for listening empathetically

■ Be quiet: which means stop talking to yourself in your head (e.g. rehearsing your next question) as well. If the other person stops talking, count to three before saying anything. If they continue talking, keep quiet.

■ Be attentive: focus all your attention on the other person. Use your voice tone, posture and eye contact to let the other person know that you are paying attention.

■ Suspend judgement: clear your mind of your own thoughts. Do not make judgements based on your own views or perceptions. Seek to understand the other person's views and perceptions before expressing your own.

■ Understanding is not necessarily agreeing: the objective is to understand, not to agree. Understanding the other person does not mean you are forced to agree with them. You can still hold your own opinion. You don't need to defend your ideas or position in order to understand the other person's.

■ Paraphrase and summarise frequently: summarise the message in your own words. *Check* with the other person that you have heard what they meant to say – that you have got the right message. Do this much more frequently than you think is necessary – it keeps you on track and demonstrates your interest and understanding. Always paraphrase before asking a question – it should flow naturally. If the question you were planning does not flow, then don't ask it!

■ Listen to feelings: share your own feelings. Pay attention to the signals (both verbal and non-verbal) that indicate what the other person might be feeling. Summarise these and *check* to see if you have guessed correctly.

■ Encourage possibilities: use open questions to encourage the other person to consider other possibilities. Do *not* give advice or state your own opinions.

---

[2] Covey, Steven (1989) *The Seven Habits of Highly Effective People*, New York, Simon & Schuster.

Ideas style

Description	People talk about:	People are:
Ideas-oriented people handle the world in terms of concepts, abstractions, theories and models. They value imagination, innovation and creativity very much. They are future oriented. Preferred type of agreement: *shared vision*. Preferred style of discourse: *inspire*.	Concepts Innovation Creativity Potential Opportunities Possibilities Grand designs Improving Interdependence What's new in the field Alternatives New methods	Imaginative Charismatic Difficult to understand Ego centred Unrealistic Creative Full of ideas Provocative

Ideas-oriented people use their responsiveness to connect with other people's values and beliefs and build exciting possibilities for the future. Outcomes of cooperation are achieved through *moving together* with the people they are trying to influence. This style is dependent on your personal ability to take the lead in putting forward your vision in an inspiring way. It is a style that does not try to influence by pushing people into action, but by attracting or pulling them.

The ideas style combines high responsiveness with high direction. It bases its influence on building strong connections with people and then directing that latent energy into a direction – a vision. It relies on generating enthusiasm and attracting people with common ground to a common vision of what might be. In that sense it is quite idealistic, so the more far-sighted the vision, the deeper the connection has to be with the other party(ies) to make sure that they come with you. It is not worth having a great vision if people are not attracted to it and don't 'buy in'. Equally, having a great connection with people is a wasted opportunity if that energy is not directed into a positive direction.

In a negotiation arena, the ideas style is useful to create a positive climate of cooperation, a vision of successful outcomes and a sense of common ground and connection. The ideas style builds **cooperation**.

Non-verbal communication

Non-verbal communication is simply communication without words. At the extreme, a mime artist or ballet dancer is conveying the whole meaning through non-verbal communication. But in most situations, non-verbal communication is an amplifier of – or detractor from – the spoken word.

The whole gambit of non-verbal communication includes gesture and touch, facial expressions, eye contact, body language, posture, dress, clothing, spatial distance, physical appearance, and the rhythm, intonation, stress and tone of voice. A lot to take in and understand whilst we are simultaneously processing the content of the verbal message!

People are able to process this wealth of information and make judgements, often sub-consciously, partly because they learn to use and understand non-verbal communication long before they learn the verbal skills. Babies learn to interpret non-verbal messages shortly after birth and young children are generally more adept at reading non-verbal cues than adults. This is due, in part, to their limited verbal skills – they know far more than they can verbalise and therefore rely on the non-verbal to communicate. Then, as verbal skills develop, the non-verbal channels of communication become a part of the total communication process, but now mostly at the sub-conscious level.

Adults consciously use non-verbal communication because they recognise that words alone have limitations. There are many times when gesture is more effective than a verbal explanation. Try describing a spiral staircase without using your hands, or giving someone directions in the street! What is not recognised is that a lot of the signals we give non-verbally express inner feelings and thoughts, and these cannot be controlled as easily as spoken words. This is where people typically come unstuck and send mixed messages to others which undermines effective communication.

The words, music and dance of communication

A famous, but not universally applicable (in his own words), piece of research by Albert Mehrabian[3] found that clues from spoken words, from the voice tone, and from the facial expression contribute 7 per cent, 38 per cent and 55 per cent respectively to the total meaning of

[3] Mehrabian, Albert (1971) *Silent Messages: Implicit communication of emotions and attitudes*, California, Wadsworth.

a message (the words, music and dance of communication – see Figure 4.3). Obviously it depends on the context – you do not understand 93 per cent of the message of someone speaking in a foreign language. But there are some important points embedded in this and other research:

- When communicating person-to-person, much of the meaning is communicated verbally, and much is communicated non-verbally.
- A lot of communication comes through non-verbally.
- When communicating feelings and attitude, the non-verbal messages are more significant (this was the focus of Mehrabian's research).
- De-coding of non-verbal information is a less conscious activity.
- When people are unsure about the content and when they trust the other person less, they pay more attention to the non-verbal messages.
- In the absence of non-verbal clues, the chances of misunderstanding the communication are higher.

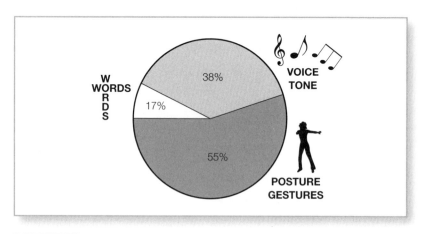

figure 4.3   The words, music and dance of communication

If you pick up messages from the music (the tone of voice and intonation of how these words are spoken) and the dance (the gestures, posture, eye contact and body language) which do not match the words (their literal meaning) there is a mixed message, and you will tend to believe the music and dance, not the words.

Why does this happen? One reason is that messages are decoded in the brain at different levels and at different speeds. Response to a lot of body language, posture and gesture is instantaneous and unconscious. It triggers a built in, automatic, survival response mechanism reaction to keep us from danger. Body language triggers a response in the 'oldest' part of the brain, often referred to as the reptilian brain. This has a primary responsibility to keep us alive and reproducing. So messages conveying aggression or gestures conveying attraction have an immediate impact. This then affects what happens next in decoding the message. Before you hear the words, or have a chance to try to understand them, you are already reacting to the other person's dance, and that is affecting your judgement.

The next level of the brain is often referred to as the limbic system. It is the emotional brain, also called the mammalian brain as its functions are shared with other mammals who can convey emotion. It helps to guide you towards pleasurable activities and away from harmful ones that you have learned through experience. So when you hear a voice tone that you connect with past experience, you link into the emotional brain and what you know of the feelings and emotions that these bring. You have now made up your mind about the context in which you will interpret what the other person is saying in their message.

The final interpretation takes place in the largest and most complex level of the brain, the neo-cortex. This is the thinking part of the brain shared only with other human beings. It is what makes humans who they are: the ability to use complex language, logic, reasoning and other higher-level processes. So the tendency is to believe that this is the dominant part of the brain. But, as you can see, by the time you are expending effort in the neo-cortex working out the language of the complex message, you have already made up your mind whether or not you believe the other person, whether or not you like them, and whether or not they are a threat to you – and a lot of subtlety in between. You decode the words in the message in this context (see Figure 4.4). Your emotions and feelings have controlled your decision.

The double-whammy comes when you send a message (see Figure 4.5). When you are thinking about sending an important message or making a presentation, you will probably spend the majority of the time writing the script (words). If you have time left, and if it is really important, you may read through the presentation to make sure you say it right (music) – though surprisingly few say the words out loud, and even fewer will rehearse with someone else in order to get feedback. Finally, a tiny number will consider their posture or body language – most will just turn up on the day and deliver their presentation cold.

figure 4.4 The sequence of decoding a message

No wonder there is so much miscommunication. People should take more notice of actors, who spend days and weeks rehearsing the words, music and dance to make sure that their message is believable by their audience.

An effective negotiator needs to be able to send clear and unambiguous messages to the other party. That means making the words, music and dance congruent, and understanding the messages being sent. An effective negotiator also needs to understand and read non-verbal messages from the other party. They give an insight to what the other party is thinking and feeling, and can be a great help in determining what is important and what is not so important.

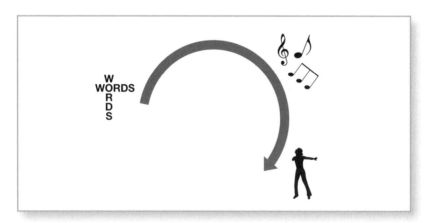

figure 4.5 The sequence of coding a message

Cultural differences in style preference

Style preferences are affected by a number of influences – education, upbringing, role models, parents, profession, gender, age, nationality – all combining to build a strong identity of 'how you do things'. Cluster people together who have similar identities, and you have a culture, whether that be a national culture; a professional culture such as sales, engineering or accountancy; an organisation culture (this is the way we do things around here); or one that is age or generation related. These different cultures have often developed a way of communicating and influencing that suits them, and this then has an impact in your influencing arena whenever you cross a barrier and try to work with someone from a different culture.

Crossing these frontiers or barriers is commonplace now with a global workforce that spans national boundaries and project working where cross-functional teams are the norm. Understanding different cultures will help you to communicate better by being able to adapt to the needs and preferences of the different cultures.

A preference for action-oriented communication can be identified in the USA, Canada, Australia and other nationalities where action and speed are of the essence. Organisations who rely on short-term decision making – fast moving consumer goods, sales, retail – will probably have a preference towards the action style. Many senior managers in organisations also prefer this style as they are rewarded for getting results.

Process-oriented communication is preferred in cultures where structure and logical decision making are paramount. Countries such as Austria, Germany, Denmark and Sweden come immediately to mind. It appeals to professions such as technology, engineering and accountancy where there is a strong reliance on a scientific and systematic methodology. Process driven organisations – oil and chemicals, pharmaceuticals, engineering, manufacturing, government – all rely on solid, data-driven problem solving, and will exhibit strong process style tendencies. Process style communication is also predominant in the way children are taught in schools, so it has a comfortable feel, even if it is not an individual preference.

People-oriented communication is the cultural norm in countries where consensus and respect for people and their ideas is important (e.g. Asia, Japan). In this culture, the relationship is more significant than the task, so it can also be identified in social science driven professions such as social work, human resources, health and education (primarily at the delivery point rather than in the management, which accounts for some of the difficult relationships in these professions between practitioners and managers).

Ideas-oriented communication is typical of cultures where it is the norm to ask questions like, 'What are the arguments for doing it this way? Why? Why not?', where people must be convinced of the substance in the message being conveyed. This is common in countries like France and in research and development and project leadership. It is a style that is attractive to some of the younger generation who want to believe in what they are doing and in the purpose behind the organisation, not just to do a job.

Communication styles and negotiation

Think back to the desired outcome for each phase of the OPEC model which determines the success of the interaction phase of a negotiation, and compare those outcomes with those of the four communication styles. A pattern emerges showing that each of the four communication styles is needed in the negotiation, and styles are directly linked to each of the OPEC phases.

In the opening phase you want to ensure cooperation with the other party, so the predominant style should be ideas. You need to highlight the common ground and connection that exists and envision a successful and positive outcome to the negotiation in order to create a positive and forward looking climate. There is a people style element to the opening phase as well, as you need to be sensitive to others and to build rapport. But the main need is for the ideas style, to build a positive atmosphere of cooperation.

In the positioning phase, the focus is on bringing in your data and analysis and making a statement about your own position or potential solution to the problem. You engage in debate and discussion with the other party, weighing up the options. The predominant style is process.

Moving to exploring, the need is to probe and listen to discover and understand the underlying needs and wants of the other party, and to share your own thinking about your needs in order to open up new possibilities and options for exchange. The best style here is people, with some use of the ideas style, especially when envisioning potential alternatives and opportunities.

Finally, when you put together the deal in the closing phase, the style will be action: the demand and exchange from both sides is the final agreement.

So, in a negotiation each one of the four styles is used in a sequence in order to get the desired result – see Figure 4.6.

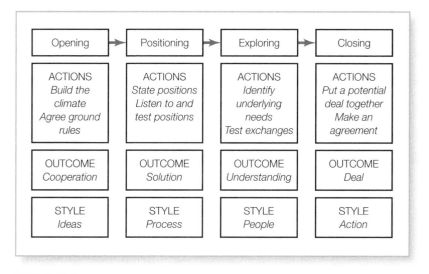

figure 4.6   The actions, outcomes and predominant style for each phase of the OPEC process

In Part 1 of this book, I have been helping you to look at the negotiation environment, the need for negotiation skills in the twenty-first century working environment, especially to resolve internal disputes in the organisation, and the importance of being flexible in our communication and interaction skills to manage each phase of the negotiation process effectively.

In Part 2, I will introduce you to the detailed steps to develop an effective plan for a negotiation and how to carry out that plan to ensure a successful outcome.

part

2

Doing it

5

Planning a negotiation

So, you have a conflict and you have decided to negotiate. Are you sure this is the right approach?

In the first chapter, I identified several different sources of conflict and several different strategies that can be used to resolve them. Later in the book you saw that entering into a negotiation process takes time, effort and a desire to collaborate with the other party concerned. Do you have the time, energy and mindset needed? Is another strategy feasible and able to deliver a positive result? If the situation is one where there is a real need to build and maintain a long-term, positive working relationship with the other party, then negotiating and collaborating is likely to be the right response. But it is not the only one.

On the other hand, you may see a situation as being a straight division of a finite resource: 'The cake is only so big, it is a matter of dividing it fairly.' Are you sure? In his 1982 book, Gavin Kennedy proposed that 'everything is negotiable', suggesting that even when we think there is no room to negotiate and get a better deal, it is possible to negotiate. A fixed sale price is not necessarily fixed, even in a major department store. For example, nearly all stores offer purchase by credit card; the store is charged a percentage of the sale by the credit card company for the facility, say 5 per cent, so they may be prepared to offer you a discount of, say 4 per cent if you pay by cash. You are getting a discount on the sale price, the store is making the sale and not having to pay the commission to the credit card company. The trick in these situations is to add more and more ingredients so that you create a bigger cake to divide. If you are in a 'one-off' situation where there is no likelihood of an on-going relationship needed with the other party, then there is less incentive to spend the time and effort to prepare and implement a negotiating strategy.

Preparing for the negotiation

Each negotiation is unique. Even if you have an on-going relationship with the other party, the circumstances of the upcoming negotiation means that it is a new situation that has not been experienced before. But, just like in project management, you can use some tried and tested tools and processes to enable you to manage these unique situations. You must not make assumptions that cause you to prepare ineffectively, so committing time to planning from the beginning in each situation is necessary.

Choosing to negotiate is a strategic decision. Having made that decision, you need to plan the interaction process to deliver success and a win–win solution. In the vast majority of real world negotiations, people do not prepare well for a negotiation. They read through the information, have a meeting with the interested parties (sometimes), agree some goals and a bottom line, and then 'see what happens on the day'. They end up with some sort of deal, but it is nearly always some form of compromise where neither party got the best they could from the time and opportunity available. Effective planning (even by one party and not the other) will massively increase the possibility of better deals and more effective use of time.

Start planning for a negotiation by gathering information and assessing the situation by using the 12-point preparation phase checklist introduced in Chapter 3 and summarised in the box below. This will help you to confirm the decision to negotiate and to define the scale and complexity of the negotiation – and therefore the time and effort needed for the planning process.

12-point Preparation Phase Checklist

1 What is the situation?

2 What is the scope?

3 What type of conflict is underlying?

4 Does this affect anything else?

5 Do you need to negotiate?

6 Who is involved?

7 How urgent are matters?

8 Where will you negotiate?

9 Are you in the public eye?

10 Any other third parties involved?

11 Who makes the decisions?

12 Who can help you?

The negotiation continuum

The first question to ask puts the negotiation planning in context. A negotiation needs to have both common and conflicting interests. How much conflict is there between the two parties? Is it going to be a simple exchange or are the issues and positions more complex? Negotiation is on a continuum of complexity from haggling at one extreme to complex negotiating at the other, depending on how significant the differences between the parties are (see Figure 5.1).

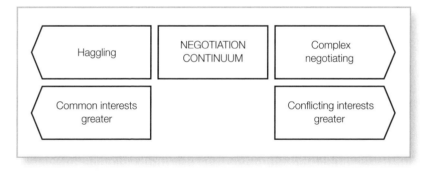

figure 5.1   **The negotiation continuum**

Problem solving

If there are no conflicting interests at all, or they are insignificant, then the two parties are in the realm of rational problem solving. The parties share the same goals and interests, they will tend to view facts objectively and rationally to find the best solution. Influence does play a part. You would like to make sure that the problem is solved effectively and that your preferred solutions are properly and fully considered. But you are open to rational debate and discussion, as there is no fundamental difference between your needs and the needs of the other party. There is no hidden agenda or conflicting interests, so there is no reason why you cannot come together and resolve the problem.

However, even in cases that look like problem solving, there may be hidden conflict. You will have attended so-called 'problem solving meetings' where the individual parties have entrenched positions that benefit them. The annual budget discussions in organisations are cases in point. They are usually billed as problem-solving meetings to agree the next year's targets and resource allocation. The proposals from each department have been put together with a great amount of attention to detail and with a high level of analysis. But the discussion soon leaves the realms of rational and open discussion and moves into attack and defence in order to obtain a proportionally higher share of the budget allocation, whether that is in the organisation's overall interest or not.

Beware also the scenario where one party thinks they are problem solving and the other party is negotiating. Take for instance an internal office reorganisation: for the office services manager it is a piece of problem solving. There are regulations, both legal and following organisation policy, regarding the space required for each person. There is the space available, it is just a matter of distributing it between the people in accordance with the specifications. For the people being moved, it is not problem solving – they have an interest in where they sit, next to whom, how close to the coffee machine, in an open area or private office. It is not problem solving to them, it is definitely a negotiation where there are conflicting interests that need to be resolved.

Haggling

Haggling is a form of negotiation called distributive negotiation. A distributive negotiation normally entails a single issue to be negotiated, usually price. It is a form of 'fixed-cake' scenario where each party discusses, proposes, argues or barters about the terms of a transaction. There is only so much of the fixed cake to discuss, and the proportions that can be distributed are also limited. A distributive negotiation often involves people who do not have a relationship, nor are they likely to do so again in the future. Buying a car or a house, or purchasing a commodity fall into this category. There is only a single issue, and you discuss the terms of the distribution of that single issue in a way that is eventually deemed 'fair' by both sides as it meets their needs.

The process of haggling is not just cutting the cake down the middle. As mentioned at the start of this chapter, you can extend the issue in most situations to create a situation where the cake is enlarged, so each party then gets a bigger slice when it is divided. So when buying a house, it is possible to speed up or delay the transaction to meet the needs for a quick or delayed sale by the vendor, and this may be worth a consideration in terms of the asking price. The seller could decide to include some furniture, fixtures and fittings that they do not wish to take and these might be worth a consideration of a higher price by the purchaser.

There is opportunity to bring in a number of related issues to the discussion that are of low cost to the provider but of high value to the receiver. This way you add more into the mix to make a bigger cake, so that when it is eventually divided, it is not just the price issue that is under discussion. The eventual deal is more robust and seen to be 'fairer' to both sides because they managed to achieve more than they initially expected on just price alone.

So haggling is a valid negotiating strategy and effective planning for the discussion is equally important when haggling. You need to discover and consider what the other person needs in addition to the price and see what options you have to provide these things at low relative cost to yourself.

Complex negotiation

The other end of the negotiation continuum is complex negotiation. This type of negotiation is usually referred to as integrative negotiation, and implies some degree of cooperation to achieve something together. This means that a higher degree of trust and a good relationship between both parties is essential. Both parties want to leave the negotiation arena feeling they've achieved something which has value by getting what each wants. Integrative negotiation involves greater emphasis on making value-for-value exchanges, which become more creative as the depth of conflict increases. Generally, integrative negotiation is seeking to form a longer-term relationship to create mutual gain than is expected in haggling. So it also warrants more time and effort.

High-complexity negotiation mirrors project management in a number of ways. It becomes more of a programme of individual projects or negotiations, all interlinked to provide an eventual agreement. So, in a merger negotiation between two companies, there will be a number of parallel discussions and negotiations taking place on the integration of activities, location of offices, product overlap, sharing of services, rationalisation of suppliers, share price, debt allocation, appointment of executives and officers, cost implications, IT integration, communication strategy, etc., some of which are conditional on other negotiated agreements, and others which can be run in parallel. It is a complex matrix of interdependent negotiations, not just the two lead negotiating teams sitting down to agree the principles and price.

Principled negotiation

Underpinning effective win–win negotiating are some fundamentals that are generally referred to as principled negotiation. This is an approach to negotiation that was first proposed in the book *Getting to Yes* by Roger Fisher and William Ury[1] and developed at the Harvard Negotiating Project. It seeks to move away from posturing and game play in a negotiation and resolve the differences on their merit and through finding opportunities for mutual gain.

There are four principles:

1 **Separate the people from the problem.** You don't have to like someone to negotiate with them, but if you don't like them it will make it very hard to be open and objective. The greater the dislike, the greater the mistrust, which will mean it will not be possible to engage for mutual benefit. (If you don't like the other person, it follows that you are not likely to want them to benefit!) So the more you can separate the problem and focus on that, the more likely you are to get to a win–win outcome. People problems also often involve difficult emotions – fear, anger, distrust and anxiety for example. These emotions get mixed up with the substantive issues and make both harder to deal with.

2 **Focus on interests not positions.** Most negotiations fail to achieve their potential and end in compromise because one party lacks the ability to move beyond positioning statements and trying to persuade the other party that its position is better/more acceptable. People mix what they want with what they need. Remember the night-time sandwich in Chapter 3? My interest – my need – in that example is to satisfy hunger. My position – my want – is for a sandwich. This will satisfy my need, but it is only one way of doing so – there may be other alternatives. In negotiations, you should try to work out the best solution and

---

[1] Fisher, Roger and Ury, William (1982) *Getting to Yes*, London, Hutchison/ Arrow Books.

propose that as your position and bargain from that point. It is a way of satisfying your need, but only one way. Engaging in positional bargaining stops you moving to understand interests and possibilities for different solutions.

3 **Invent options for mutual gain.** Once you have moved away from positions to interests, then more options start to emerge which are potential exchanges. Opportunities arise for mutual gain, where the cost to one side is lower than the value to the other side; or for future collaboration which could reduce or eliminate the source of the conflict. Fisher and Ury describe an argument between two sisters over an orange. Both want the orange and can't decide on who should have it, so they compromise and halve it. Then one sister eats the flesh of her half and throws away the peel, while the other sister cuts off the peel to use in her baking, and throws away the flesh. There is an opportunity here for mutual gain where both sisters get what they need, and can avoid arguments in the future. Most business discussions are more complex, but often the solutions are just as simple.

4 **Insist on objective criteria.** Often in negotiations there is argument over differences that become a battle of wills between each side mostly based on perceptions, assumptions and opinions. While not always available, if some outside, objective criteria for fairness can be found, this can greatly simplify the negotiation process. Contracts can be based on what other similar companies have agreed to use. Prices can be measured against market conditions and norms. Stated opinions can be checked for assumptions and underlying objectivity. This gives both sides more independent guidance on what constitutes 'fair'.

Five steps to plan a negotiation

The planning steps for a negotiation implement these four principles and aim to reduce the possibility of ending in a win–lose situation. There are five steps required to develop a plan, as shown in Figure 5.2. They follow a sequence that ensures that all aspects of the upcoming negotiation are considered, and any uncertainties or difficulties are identified so that plans can be put in place to minimise or eliminate their potential negative impact on the outcome. Each of the five steps has a number of tools to help complete that step successfully. Once the step has been completed, the outcome can be summarised on the one-page negotiation planning guide shown at the end of the chapter in Figure 5.8.

1. What is the issue?
2. Who are the parties involved?
3. What does each party want and have to offer?
4. What strategy should we use?
5. Where do we start?

figure 5.2   **The five steps to plan a negotiation**

Step 1:   What is the issue?

The issue may be obvious to both parties, as in a purchasing or labour dispute situation, but it is always worthwhile checking your assumptions to make sure that there is a clear issue, and that both parties recognise it and the need to negotiate an outcome. There may be other issues that are involved which, if not clearly identified at the outset, may create problems later in the negotiation. Union and labour disputes are often subject to 'issue creep' during a negotiation, when some of the conflicts and tensions that have been simmering unnoticed suddenly surface and unsettle the negotiation. It is better to think through the issue before engaging with the other party to make sure that there are no surprises, and also that you plan for the right negotiation. Sometimes the presenting issue is not the right issue to negotiate.

It also pays dividends to take time to define the issue when there are more long-term relationship goals. You might need to negotiate strategic alliances with stakeholders or decision makers in advance of a substantive negotiation on the terms of a long-term partnership. In highly political and complex negotiations you might need to negotiate the issue to be discussed, where the meeting will take place, even the layout of the meeting room and the seating plan of the participants. All of these meetings and negotiations that take place prior to the main negotiation should be planned and implemented individually, as the circumstances, context, personnel involved and timing are all different and unique. Each needs to be completed before the next negotiation in the sequence can begin, and the planning for subsequent negotiations is affected by the preceding ones.

In such complex situations it is worthwhile utilising stakeholder analysis[2] and project management tools to ensure the correct sequence and the right people are involved in each negotiation.

---

[2] A number of stakeholder analysis tools can be found in my 2010 book, *Getting Results Without Authority*.

Example

Leonard works in the technology industry. One of his key customers is developing a new product and has asked Leonard's company to bid to be a partner in that activity. It would be a significant contract for Leonard's company, who have a good relationship with the other company, based on small-scale contracts over a period of time. This contract would be a significant expansion of the business.

In his planning process, Leonard maps the stakeholders in the customer organisation who will have an impact on the decision to award the contract. Some of the stakeholders he knows well, others only by reputation, so he brings together information by talking to colleagues in the account team and others who have had dealings with this customer. What could he do to better ensure success in the contract negotiation?

His first analysis was positive – most of the key decision makers seemed to be on their side. The company had a great relationship with the engineering group in the customer organisation for whom this technology was destined. There was also a strong relationship with the chief buyer for the group, who had requested the bid, and had always expressed a preference for Leonard's company over its competitors.

However, the stakeholder analysis identified three key decision influencers for this new contract where there was not such a positive feeling. In particular, the technical manager in the customer's company was new in post. She had previously held a senior position as a key technical lead in one of Leonard's competitors, and this competitor was also bidding for the contract. She could be a real threat as she could favour her previous company, no-one in the team had an established relationship with her, and any previous relationship had been one of mistrust and competition when she was in the rival company.

Based on this analysis, Leonard decided that a first priority had to be to negotiate a better relationship with the technical manager. A lot of their thinking about her was based on reputation and expectations that she would favour her previous employer. He needed to check these assumptions, find out her needs and explore ways of making sure that these could be satisfied in the eventual contract negotiations. Negotiating a better relationship with the technical manager was the first step; based on the outcome of that negotiation, he could then plan to meet with the chief buyer and the customer team to negotiate the terms of the proposed partnership contract.

Step 2:   Who are the parties involved?

Having defined the parties to the negotiation and the issue, the next planning step is to identify the personalities and roles involved. To be successful, the people and the problem need to be separated, so this step helps to identify any people issues that have to be addressed so that the negotiation can focus properly on the negotiation issues. There are two basic questions: Who am I? and 'Who are you?' (see Figure 5.3).

WHO AM I? Name:
Describe the situation and your role in it. What is your preferred style? What are your feelings and thoughts about the other party and their organisation? What are your common interests?

WHO ARE YOU? Name:
Put yourself in the position of the other person. Describe the situation and their role in it. What is their preferred style? What are their feelings and thoughts about you and your organisation? What are their common interests?

figure 5.3   Who am I? Who are you?

What are your own thoughts and feelings as they apply to this situation and your role in it, and your thoughts and feelings about the other party. What is your natural negotiating style? What is your preferred communication style? What is the history of negotiating with the other party? Think of anything that may have an impact on the assumptions and frame of reference that you create for the situation. It is important that you do this afresh for each negotiation as your analysis may be different for the same person in different situations – the role you each play will change, your relationship may be closer, the environment will have changed from previously, the source of conflict will be different. So it is important to identify the specific thoughts and feelings with the situation in mind, and not rely on previous analyses.

Then go through the same analysis for the other party. Use your knowledge of the other party to make the best decision you can – and also note where you have gaps in your knowledge that stop you being able to make a judgement. Do your research by finding out as much as possible from other sources where you do not have the level of information you would like. This analysis might identify significant gaps in information or uncover sources of conflict that suggest you need to go back to step 1, redefine the issue for negotiation and plan for that.

Some other areas to consider in this step:

■ Don't forget that you and the other party are representing an organisation as well as being yourselves. The history of the relationship between the organisations is important, and will have an impact on the negotiation. What is the reputation and culture of each organisation – is there a style of negotiation?

■ Are you or the other party negotiating as a team. If so, you need to analyse who each person in the team is on both sides. What will be the impact of the team on the negotiation (we will look at the dynamics of team negotiations in a later chapter)?

■ Is status important? In some negotiations, it is important to ensure that you have the right level of person representing the organisation. If the other party is represented by a general manager, then your side needs someone of similar status. In other situations and cultures, status may not be so important.

■ Does each party have the authority to negotiate and agree? If not, who else is involved? These stakeholders need to be considered at this step.

This step should define the common interests that exist in the negotiation scenario, and identify any underlying emotional or personal issues that could jeopardise a successful outcome.

Step 3: What does each party want and have to offer?

Win–win negotiation is based on 'exchanging ideas and propositions in order to reach an agreement', so this step is about defining what it is that each party wants from the negotiation and what each has in its control to give in exchange.

Wants, needs and haves

Wants

The first activity is to list all of the wants from both perspectives – yours and the other party's. What are the priorities of these wants? If you try to negotiate on too many fronts, try to pursue too many objectives at the same time, you may well confuse yourself and the other person and not achieve your main goal – so identify the priorities. Your wants may be tangible (a resource, money, data, product, etc.) or more intangible (support, understanding, commitment, acceptance, etc.). List all of them if they are important to you or the other party.

When considering from the other party's perspective you may have to make a judgement based on your knowledge and understanding. If you find that you are unable to identify wants and haves from the other side, it may indicate that you need to go back a step or two in the process, as you don't know enough about the other party to be able to define the issue or do any planning. You will be going into a negotiation in pure reaction mode, which is not satisfactory. So you may need to redefine the issue for an initial negotiation, or do further research.

Needs

Before moving on to thinking about what you and the other party has to exchange, you need to identify the underlying need, or needs, driving this negotiation. What need is driving your wants? What is the 'hunger' to your 'sandwich'? What need must be satisfied to make this negotiation a success?

Wants and needs are like an inverted iceberg – we see a lot of things we would like to have – our wants. These are above the surface. But the needs that are driving these wants, and especially the prime, basic need, are below the waterline, so not easily identified (see Figure 5.4).

One of the best ways to identify the needs that are driving what we want is to use a tool from problem root cause analysis – the five whys. The five whys is a simple problem-solving technique that helps you to get to the root of a problem quickly, and can equally be applied to basic need analysis. This tool involves looking at any problem and asking 'Why?' and 'What caused this problem?' as often as necessary to get to the root cause – which is when you can't answer the question any more. (The number five in the title 'five whys' is not fixed, you ask as many times as necessary.) To translate this tool for basic need analysis, ask the questions 'Why is this want important to us?', 'Why do I want this?', 'What need does this satisfy?' as many times as necessary. Then you will get towards a basic need which has to be satisfied in order for the negotiation to be successful.

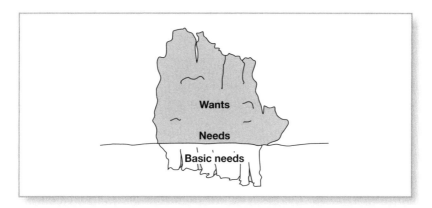

figure 5.4 Wants and needs – the upside down iceberg

A note about needs

As humans we are motivated by the desire for satisfaction of our needs. Abraham Maslow identified that these needs are organised in a hierarchy, with lower level needs being the strongest and having to be satisfied before higher level needs come into play. So a basic need in a negotiation could be survival or security driven (e.g. if we don't conduct this deal my job is at stake or my organisation will not survive) which would be indicative of lower level needs. Or the basic need could be driven by social, status or ego needs (e.g. I want to be seen to be competent/I need to cooperate/we need to be seen as important players in the industry) which would be indicative of higher level needs.

The deeper it is possible to go down the upside down iceberg, the more options are available. In the sandwich example, if, at the want level, you want a cheese sandwich, then only a cheese sandwich would satisfy; if you want a sandwich, then there are more options of different fillings for the sandwich; if the need is something to eat, then other options quickly become obvious; and at the basic need level of satisfying hunger/survival, the options are even more numerous. Obviously, when looking at the other party's basic needs, it is not possible to predict with certainty what is driving them personally or organisationally, but the better the relationship and the better your knowledge of their situation, the more you can predict possible motivations which can then be tested out in the negotiation arena (especially during the exploring phase).

Haves

An understanding of wants and needs allows us to then list all that you have in your control that is of value to the other party that you could exchange: your 'haves'. And to list all of the 'haves' from the other party's perspective – what they control that is of value to you and that will satisfy your wants and needs. See Figure 5.5.

What do I want?	**What do you want?**
List all the things you would like to get out of this negotiation. What are your priorities? Identify your need – what must you have in order for the negotiation to be successful?	List all the things you think the other party would like to get out of this negotiation. What are their priorities? Identify their needs – what must they have in order for the negotiation to be successful?
What do I have?	**What do you have?**
List all the things that you have the power to give in exchange. What do you have that might be of value to the other party? List everything you have – you can decide later whether or not you give it.	List all the things that you think that the other party has the power to give in exchange. What do they have that might be of value to you? List everything you can think of – whether or not you think they will give it.

figure 5.5   What do I want and have? What do you want and have?

Again, it is best to start with the long list, and not forget to include the obvious 'haves'. The more options that can be identified on both sides, the greater the possibility of finding exchanges that work in the negotiation. At this stage you are not committing to offer what you have listed – you can decide at the time whether it should form part of the package. The same applies to planning from the other party's perspective – make the long list, whether you think they will be prepared to give you something or not, and don't omit the obvious ones.

Note that in Figure 5.5, I have drawn the 'Want' boxes diagonally opposite to the 'Have' boxes, making it easy to compare the two. There should be some matches in the two boxes which will help you to formulate an opening position and possible exchanges that will lead to agreement.

Step 4:   What strategy should we use?

There are two major questions that determine your overall strategy in a negotiation. You are committed to a collaborative approach in order to achieve a win–win result, but you need to take account of the power balance and your relationship with the other party in order to make sure that you follow an approach that will lead to mutual benefit and a positive outcome.

Power balance

The first question is about power balance. Most sellers think that buyers have the greater amount of power, especially when economic activity is low. So they reduce price in order to sell. Yet research of buying decisions shows that 80 per cent of contracts are awarded to someone other than the lowest bidder. Clearly buyers are interested in more than price, so there are other elements in the power balance to consider.

There are two realities about power: power is relative, and power is subjective – it is all in our perception. In a negotiation, if power is in your favour, then there is an opportunity to steam-roller the other party into submission and impose your terms. If you feel power is with the other party, then the tendency will be to cave in to their demands. Both lead to win–lose outcomes.

In negotiations where participants share relatively equal perceived power, parties will share more information, and the outcome will be more win–win. Research has shown that equalising the perceived power in a negotiation does not affect your relative 'take' in the negotiation, so it is in your interest to set up conditions where both parties feel they have an equal voice, feel there is relatively equal power, and can create as many resources as possible.[3]

What do you feel is the current power balance? Is it in your favour? In the other party's favour? More or less balanced? What can you do to ensure that the perceived power balance is balanced? Do you need to build your own power? Do you need to build the other party's perceived power?

---

[3] Wolfe, Rebecca and McGinn, Kathleen (2005) 'Perceived Relative Power and its Influence on Negotiations', *Harvard Management Update*, September.

What can you do to affect the power balance?

- Increasing the number of haves at your and the other party's disposal. Having more options builds power.

- Knowing your and the other party's basic need allows you to generate more creative solutions and increase power.

- Having a good alternative to the negotiation – a BATNA (see the box below) – builds your power by giving you a credible option to an agreement in this negotiation.

- Planning well increases power as it makes you better prepared for any development. Planning well from the other party's perspective means you can help them with their side of the bargaining if they feel the power balance is in your favour.

- Having skills as a communicator and negotiator allows you to build relative power, by being able to put your case well and also ensuring that you do not overpower the other party.

- Following the OPEC phase structure in the interaction means that you keep yourself and the other party on a track which leads to win–win.

A note about BATNA

It is an acronym for the 'Best Alternative To a Negotiated Agreement' developed by Roger Fisher and William Ury in their book *Getting to Yes*. It is the alternative action that you have available should the negotiation result fail to reach a suitable agreement. If the potential results of the negotiation offers a value that is less than your BATNA, there is no point in proceeding; you take your best available alternative option (your BATNA) instead. For example, a BATNA to buying a new, larger house could be extending your current house.

Strategic approach

The second question is to decide your overall approach to the relationship with the other party. This means setting an overall strategic approach to how you will behave towards the other party in the negotiation. Many negotiators aim to react to the behaviour of the other party during the interaction, waiting to see how the other person reacts and responding accordingly. This approach has two dangers:

■ Firstly, you have not planned your responses, so you could be caught unawares by an approach taken by the other party, and it means that you can only be reactive in the negotiation. You have handed the initiative to the other party to control the style and pace of the negotiation.

■ Secondly, you risk sending mixed messages to the other party about your intentions. A lack of preparation will mean that you will naturally begin the negotiation in defensive and questioning mode – waiting for clues about the other party's strategy before committing to yours. Yet you may wish to build the relationship with the other party and should be taking a much more friendly and open approach. Moving to this later will send a mixed message to the other party about your intentions and commitment.

In my experience, there are two relationship issues to take into account: current and future. If your current relationship is good – trusting, open and cooperative – then you will be open and welcoming to the other party, trusting and accepting what they say to you. On the other hand, if your current relationship is poor, then you are likely to be less trusting of the other party's statements, be questioning and sceptical of them, and take a more closed stance to them. Then, projecting towards future relationship needs, you could work hard to develop a better future relationship with the other party, or you could decide that this is not important (either because it is already good, or it is not a significant requirement to have a better relationship for the future). If you want to develop the relationship with the other party, then you are likely to be more accommodating to their needs, and more flexible with your own demands. If you feel that you don't need to develop the relationship further in this negotiation, then you can take a much firmer, assertive stance.

As you will see from these different positions that you can take, it is really important that you do not radically change your position during the negotiation. If you suddenly move or fluctuate between being assertive and accommodating, it looks as though you are playing a game of 'bad cop, good cop' with the other party, and this will certainly lower trust and lessen the relationship. Hence the need to decide your overall strategic approach now, as part of planning.

When you are making your judgements about relationship, they will be subjective and based on feelings, but as most of our behaviour is controlled by our feelings (as I showed in Chapter 4), these subjective judgements are important. Both judgements on current and future relationships you are making are continuums: you place your feeling somewhere along the line between two extremes. If you are considering a brand new relationship with someone, then you need to start on the side of being less trusting than with one where you already have some information, but it does not have to be at the extreme. You can conduct research on the other party and their organisation to discover their reputation and relationships with others, so that you just need to err on the side of caution in the initial exchanges.

A combination of these two judgements on current and future relationship needs gives you four main interaction strategies to choose from, as shown in Figure 5.6.

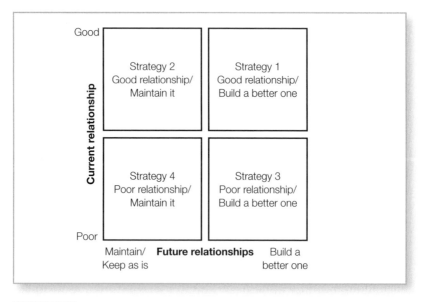

figure 5.6 Four strategic negotiation approaches

Strategy 1: Good relationship/Build a better one

You have a good current relationship but it is also important to invest energy into building an even better future relationship. You want to develop the partnership even further and deeper.

Your interaction strategy for the whole negotiation will therefore be guided by principles of openness towards the other party and trusting of the information they provide and their motives, based on the good relationship that currently exists. You will also want to follow an approach that tries to be accommodating towards their needs, and in which you show flexibility in your demands, both of which will sustain the good relationship you have and build an even better relationship for the future.

Strategy 2: Good relationship/Maintain it

You have a good current relationship and but it is not important to invest energy into building an even better future relationship. This may be in a situation where the detail of the agreement is important, and implementation is not dependent on an improved relationship, for example negotiating a supply schedule in an existing framework agreement.

In this situation, you will still have an interaction strategy which is open and trusting; but you can afford to be less accommodating and more assertive when it comes to responding to the other party's needs and putting forward your own position. You want to ensure that you maintain the current, good relationship with the other party, but you do not need a better one at this time.

Strategy 3: Poor relationship/Build a better one

You have a poor current relationship with the other party, and it is important to build a better one for the future. For example, a negotiation with a supplier or contractor with whom you have no prior relationship experience where you identify the potential to build a mutually beneficial partnership beyond this negotiation.

As there is a poor current relationship, you cannot afford to be too open and trusting of the other party until you have gained information on how they will respond and react. So your interaction strategy will be more cautious and closed towards them and sceptical and questioning of what they say and their motives. But, in order to indicate your desire to build a better future relationship with them, you will show that you can be accommodating towards their needs, and show flexibility in your demands and position.

Strategy 4: Poor relationship/Maintain it

You have a relatively poor current relationship with the other party, and you do not think it is important to build a better one for the future. This could be a situation where you are making a spot purchase or a short-term deal, where you still want to have a win–win outcome and have the opportunity to negotiate in the future in a positive light, but you do not see the need to build more of a partnership at this time. Therefore, you will be more cautious and closed in your approach, and more questioning and sceptical of the other party. You can also afford to be less accommodating and more assertive when it comes to responding to the other party's needs and putting forward your own position.

Step 5:   Where do we start?

A negotiation will involve some bargaining and trading to achieve a mutually successful settlement. So where do you start? What is your expectation? And what is your limit? What are the limits and expectations of the other party? This determines the bargaining range, sometimes called the contracting zone or ZOPA – zone of possible agreement. It is the range or area in which an agreement is satisfactory to both parties involved and is essentially the overlap area in the low and high range that each party is willing to pay or find acceptable in a negotiation. The greater the bargaining range, the easier it is to reach an agreement (see Figure 5.7).

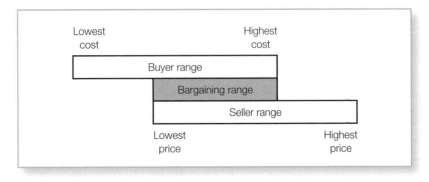

figure 5.7   **Bargaining range**

The final question in planning the strategy for a negotiation is to determine your own goals, limits and starting point. The previous planning steps will have helped you to think about and determine these. Now is the time to put some data together:

What is your goal?

This should be challenging but achievable. If the market range for houses in your area is £200,000–£250,000, then a goal of £200,000 is probably achievable, but not challenging (unless you house is in need of a lot of repair). A goal of £350,000 would be challenging, but probably not achievable. Market conditions will have an impact, but so will what else you can bring into the equation to make your house more attractive to a buyer – adding perceived value.

Another factor in setting a challenging but achievable goal is the evidence from Chester Karrass' research that negotiators who ask for more and expect more, get more.[4] Most of us tend to set our goals too low, but if you go too high, then there is a greater risk of getting no deal.

Taking this into account, what is your challenging but achievable goal? Bear in mind that it is possible to reassess your goal in the light of information that may emerge during the negotiation.

What are your limits?

In financial terms, what is the lowest price you can offer and not make a loss? What is the highest price you can pay and absorb the costs? Outside of financial considerations, what are the other fundamental elements to this negotiation that have to be there otherwise there can be no deal?

Setting your limits does two things. Firstly, it gives you clarity on your options and enables you to make better and quicker decisions during a negotiation. This will save a lot of wasted time and effort. Secondly, it prevents unacceptable positions from the other side going unchallenged when tabled – once a position is 'on the table' it gains some form of legitimacy and it is then difficult to remove. This helps you to avoid agreeing to a bad deal.

Your lower limit is your 'walk-away' position. Unless you can get the other party to move from a position which is outside your walk-away limit, continuing a negotiation is not worthwhile as it will not result in an acceptable agreement.

What is your opening?

People are often quite anxious about their opening position. Going back to the house purchase example, how much above your goal do you need to put your asking price? People fear that if they set it too high, then they will scare off potential buyers; if they set it too low they may end up getting less than they hoped for. In making an offer

---

[4] Karrass, Chester (1992) *The Negotiating Game*, revised edn., New York, Harper Business.

there is equal anxiety: if you make it too low, you risk an outright rejection and failure to proceed; if you make it too high, you may end up paying more than you wanted to.

However, if you have done your preparation on your goals and limits well, it should be an easy task. What you are doing is stating what you are looking for in the negotiation (in your ideal scenario). You will expect to come down from this opening position towards your goal or expectation range during the negotiation, so it is just your opening.

How far you set the opening from your expectation will depend on a number of factors – the market, your expectations for the negotiation, what you know of the other party's needs and expectations, the relative value of what is on offer . . . You just need to decide how much negotiating room you want to leave yourself. The interaction strategy in the last planning step you have chosen will help. If you feel you will need to be more flexible with your position or offer to satisfy your need to build a future relationship, then you will want to have some leeway. If a future relationship is not important, then you can set your opening with less leeway and be more assertive and firm in your approach.

Instead of worrying about setting the right opening position, why not wait until the other party makes their offer and then react accordingly? This is tempting but it is a dangerous trap, for two reasons. Firstly, it shows that you have not done your preparation properly – you should not need the other party to set out the bargaining range. Secondly, it suggests you are looking to win as much as you can, rather than win as much as you need – more of a win–lose strategy than a genuine collaboration approach. You are negotiating from greed not need. Opening the bidding also suggests getting a better deal for yourself. In his research, Adam Galinsky of Northwestern's Kellogg School of Management found that the final outcome of a negotiation is affected by whether the buyer or the seller makes the first offer.[5] Specifically, when a seller makes the first offer, the final settlement price tends to be higher than when the buyer makes the first offer.

All of these planning steps can be summarised in the one-page planning guide shown in Figure 5.8.

---

[5] Galinsky, Adam (2004) 'Should You Make the First Offer?' *HBS Negotiation*, July.

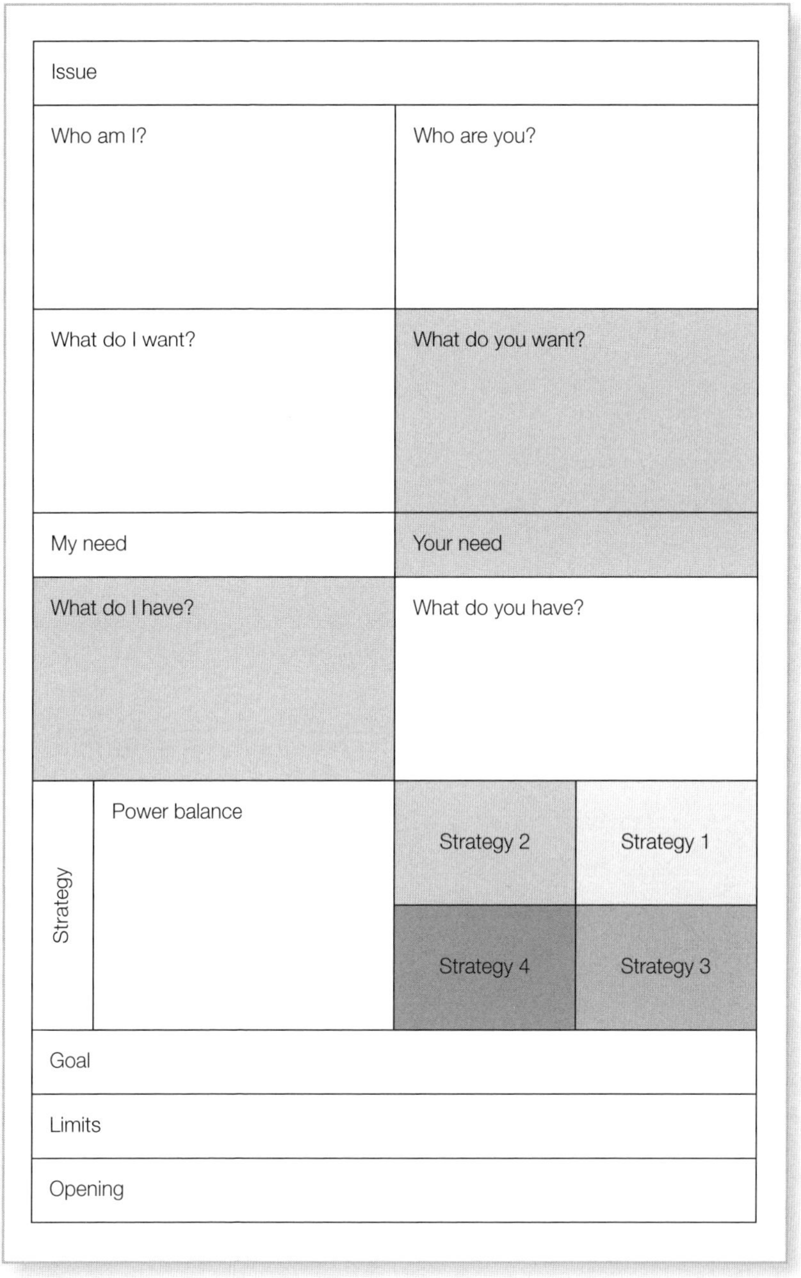

Issue	
Who am I?	Who are you?
What do I want?	What do you want?
My need	Your need
What do I have?	What do you have?

Strategy	Power balance	Strategy 2	Strategy 1
		Strategy 4	Strategy 3

Goal
Limits
Opening

figure 5.8   A negotiation planning guide

You are now ready to negotiate. In the next chapter I will look at the interaction process – OPEC – in more detail and discuss the communication issues in the negotiation arena. How do you set the right climate, get your message across, listen effectively, identify opportunities and build an agreement?

6

Conducting the negotiation

Having planned and prepared the negotiation and completed the planning guide, the next phase is interaction, when you engage with the other party or parties and follow the OPEC phases and actions to manage the negotiation arena (see Figure 6.1). In conducting the negotiation you must use your communication and interaction skills to set the right climate; get your message across clearly; listen effectively to the other party to understand their needs and expectations; test alternative exchanges with them; and put together a clear and unambiguous final agreement that is then easy to implement.

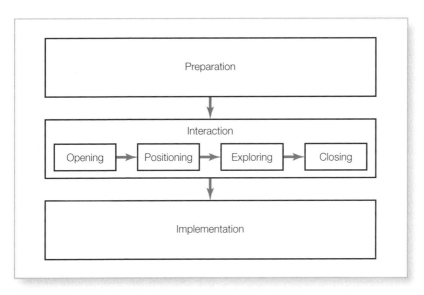

figure 6.1   Phases of a negotiation

Using the OPEC process model

The OPEC model as outlined in Figure 6.2 summarises the interaction phase from start to finish, and by completing each of the actions in the OPEC phases successfully and efficiently, you will achieve the best mutually achievable result with the other party. In this chapter, I use the four communication styles model introduced in Chapter 4 and highlight the interaction skills and approaches at each step of the OPEC process to ensure that the negotiation outcome is as good as it can be.

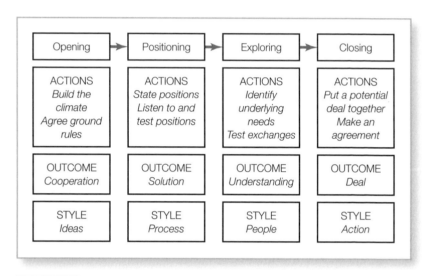

figure 6.2 The OPEC process model

Opening phase

In the opening phase there are two key actions:

- Build the climate
- Agree ground rules.

Build the climate

The first thing to point out here is that you start to build the climate long before you sit down together in the negotiating arena. Every inter-action, and lack of interaction, that takes place prior to the negotiation begins to create the climate for the discussions. If you ignore someone in the office, whether intentional or not, and then sit in a negotiation with them the next day, they will already have developed a negative impression of you. However small that is, it is a hurdle that you must overcome in order to build a positive climate for the negotiation.

Past history is relevant, as are any rumours, resentments and feelings. You will know how quickly ill-feeling grows and attitudes become entrenched in industrial and political disputes, often based on nothing more than rumour and mistrust. So, managing all interaction in a positive way in order to promote good relationships improves your ability to enter into a negotiation that will have a successful outcome. If there are bad feelings, mistrust and negative messages, your ability to deal with these in a proactive, open, non-judgemental and non-critical way will be seen as a positive sign of a better future climate for the discussions.

Starting the interaction

You can build the climate at the start of the meeting by greeting the other party positively. How much better the feeling in the room will be if you say, 'Hi, how nice to see you again. I'm really looking forward to exploring our differences today and getting a really positive outcome for both of us' (as long as it is genuine!) rather than, 'OK. Shall we get down to business. It's a difficult agenda and we have some serious problems to solve if we are going to get close to a decision.'

So, at the start of the negotiation actively plan to build the climate by consciously spending time on relationship building using the people and ideas style (see Chapter 4). Show an interest in the other party's business and any issues they are facing outside of the subject of the negotiation, share your business situation, share your expectations and goals; listen to the other party's expectations and goals; surface any issues that need to be aired before you can get down to the substance of the negotiation; express the common ground that exists between you; express positive expectations of success and envision a mutually beneficial agreement, etc.

My experience in the business world is that you shouldn't worry that you are spending too much time in building the climate. The levels of sharing, listening and of expressing positive emotions in most organisations are woefully inadequate and leave substantial room for improvement. I have noticed that people in organisations (driven by ever increasing pressures and urgency) have a strong tendency – even more so when we use email, telephone or video conferences – to leave out these social, rapport and climate building exchanges in the mistaken belief that they don't have time. In fact, the extra time that is taken later on fixing the misunderstandings that then occur and overcoming the effects of the lack of a positive working relationship is testament to the fallacy of the 'waste of time' argument.

Location, layout and seating

The layout and seating of the area where you meet will have a significant impact on the climate. It is so significant that international and political negotiations often start with a long series of detailed and painstaking negotiations on location, shape of the table and the seating arrangements. If you have control over the environment, it is worth considering the different feelings that can be created with different locations and layouts and making sure you select the most appropriate one for the negotiation you are planning.

Playing at home may be an advantage or a disadvantage. You have everything you need to hand, you are close to support, and you are in control of the environment. But, you are also affecting the power balance by using your positional power to define location, and the other party is likely to be less comfortable. Playing away also has its pros and cons. You are putting the power balance the other way, and have an opportunity to build a more positive climate. But you are further away from your support system, and you have little control over the environment. A neutral location may be the best choice in many circumstances to demonstrate no favour to either side.

The room itself is important. You create an impression on the other party with the whole environment – clean and welcoming, or noisy and hard to find. Light has a major impact on people. Daylight is best for keeping us awake and fresh. Lighting needs to be warm and effective – and not shining directly into people's faces! Space can relax or oppress. There are likely to be some elements of confidentiality so the room should be private. People also need space to breathe and not feel cramped.

The layout of the room also affects the climate. Tables are barriers but people often feel safer with a table in front of them, and they usually need something to rest papers on. The shape of the table is important. Round tables have no priority seating areas, so are seen as more equal and informal. Long tables are more formal and have a place for a neutral chairperson. Square tables have corners you can sit across. Small tables at the side of chairs create an informal environment.

Informal chairs relax you and a sofa removes all barriers (which may be appropriate). Formal chairs create a more formal atmosphere and are easier to move. How you sit will affect the climate enormously. If you sit directly opposite the other person, face-to-face, it is a classic confrontational setting. This may be appropriate for formal situations but it will also create an environment where sharing and collaboration is more difficult as the energy in the room is always being directed against or at the other person. Sitting behind your own desk, which is located at the far end of the room, is not the ideal layout to create a friendly atmosphere! The most appropriate positioning for business-like, collaborative conversation is with bodies angled, often at 90 degrees to one another. This avoids confrontation whilst still allowing easy eye contact. Sitting across a corner of a table gives this position-ing. An even more collaborative seating position is side-by-side. This is particularly useful if you want to work together on something or create the feeling of moving in harmony and together with the other party.

If you are not in control of the environment, you may be able to influence the seating arrangements by moving chairs and taking up a specific position in the room provided by your host. In many cases, such as very formal or structured negotiations, the seating plan and layout is fixed, so changing it is not possible. In these circumstances be aware of the potential impact on your behaviour of the seating and layout. The layout may also be designed to put you at a disadvantage by the other party using some tactic aimed at giving them an advan-tage and, whilst you may not be in a position to change it, you can guard against responding inappropriately. (I will address the issue of 'dirty tricks' in Chapter 8).

Agree ground rules

This action focuses on agreeing the issue that you want to discuss, and clarifying any requirements from either side regarding the agenda, timetable, form of agreement, etc. so that you can contently progress into the negotiation in a spirit of cooperation. Once again the primary communication styles are people (sharing and listening) and ideas (connecting and envisioning).

An agenda for the negotiation is important, especially when there are a number of issues to be discussed. Often these issues will be inter-related and sometimes dependent on each other, so it is important to make sure that you approach them in the right sequence. It is better to agree on the specification of product, availability and delivery capac-ity before discussing price if the supply is more dependent on quality and time rather than price.

Agreeing an agenda is another opportunity to build a positive, col-laborative working relationship with the other party. What do they want to see on the agenda? What issues would they like to discuss? What order do they want to tackle them? What are their timetable and deadlines? You can build an agenda together and that way signal your intention to collaborate and subtly indicate that you see power balanced between you. Once again, in more complex and difficult negotiations, agreeing an agenda is a negotiation in its own right.

Making sure that there is an agreement on the timetable for discussions is another opportunity to set up the meeting for success by envisioning what would be achieved in that time, and what would then be achieved in further meetings, should they be required. It also means that there is transparency on each other's deadlines for an agreement. This may appear to give a potential advantage to the other side, who could exploit your deadline by delaying tactics, putting more pressure on you to agree to a deal that is not in your favour. But the credibility and trust that you build by being prepared to take this risk nearly always pays dividends.

Some ground rules are assumed, especially where the negotiators are used to the environment and the process of negotiating. However, even in these situations it is nearly always worthwhile checking agreement to process ground rules, without being patronising: one person speaks at a time; respect for each other's position; listen; seek to understand the other person's point of view; and confidentiality. Some ground rules are implicit in the definition of win–win negotiating: collaboration; seeking win–win outcomes; engaging with intent to find an agreement; not playing games; being prepared to share and listen; and taking into account the other party's interests. Other ground rules will be specific to the situation: for example, who talks for each side (in team negotiation you also need to agree ground rules for the internal relationships); do contributions go 'through the chair'; who can call a time out or recess; what is the role of translators; who takes notes and minutes (if anyone); and who can make statements to the external world?

The final ground rule that should be discussed is the form of agreement that both parties need, assuming the conclusion of a successful negotiation. Transparency and expectations are the key important elements again – unexpectedly bringing in a team of lawyers at the contracting stage of the agreement is not a good signal of trust. Similarly, insisting on having something in writing when the other party assumed a handshake would be enough risks losing the goodwill built during the discussions. Discussing the form of agreement is a great opportunity to share expectations and show reciprocation and concern to meet the other party's needs. It also has a more subtle effect in that it is stating a clear assumption that you expect to reach an agreement – another opportunity to envision success and foster collaboration.

Having created the climate and agreed the ground rules, you can then move on to the next phase of the OPEC process – that is if the other party is also ready to move. Before moving into another phase, which involves a change of communication style and a change of focus, it is always worthwhile getting agreement to the move. This not only signals the change in the process so that it is not a sudden shock to the other party, but also allows the other party not to proceed if they are uncomfortable. It should be your intention in moving from the opening phase that both you and the other party feel that it is fine to move on to the more substantive discussion of the issue, so you can articulate this by summarising, restating the common ground that you see is the connecting element between you, envisioning the success of moving forward and getting the acceptance of the other party to join you in the next phase. If there is a reluctance to move on, then the climate is not right or the ground rules not clear, so to proceed would be fruitless. Stay in the opening phase a little longer and deal with the other party's concerns.

Positioning phase

In the positioning phase there are two key actions:

■ State positions
■ Listen to and test positions.

The positioning phase is characterised by the use of process style communication. It is a rational and logical discussion where both parties argue their opening offers and test the merits and strength of each other's positions.

State positions

In planning your negotiation (Chapter 5) you will have identified your opening offer. Exchanging your opening offers is the purpose of the first action step in positioning. Getting the opening offers on the table identifies the gap that exists between the two sides and defines the bargaining range that exists. If there is a very small gap, then an agreement is likely to be easy. The wider the gap, the more effort and skill required to reach an agreement. If there is no apparent bargaining range – each side's opening offer is beyond the walk-away position of the other – then the negotiation must stop here and the negotiators go away to reconsider their opening offers in the light of the new information, or initiate their BATNA (best alternative to a negotiated agreement).

In the rare (but not wholly unknown) event that both parties' opening offers match each other, there is no need for further discussion and a deal can be done, there and then. It is important to be alive to the possibility that there can be an immediate deal. In my experience, a number of negotiators do not see the potential for an immediate deal when it appears before them, as they slavishly follow the script of their sales pitch, or follow their plan. On one occasion, a car salesman was so intent on his sales pitch that he ignored my clear, repeated buying signals – 'I want to buy a five-door, maroon, manual gearbox with fuel injection, at my company's agreed discount price, but what is the delivery date?' – and I had to interrupt him on several occasions to get him to give me a delivery date instead of showing me the models, the different colour ways, introducing me to the maintenance manager, and wanting me to take a test drive. If you are not attuned to the possibility of an early agreement, you will not notice it when it appears, and you may snatch defeat from the jaws of victory!

In putting across your own opening position, you want to deliver your message clearly and confidently. This is process style communication, so propose precisely and reason concisely. State your proposal and back it up with your reasoning. The more your reasoning can take into account the needs and expectations of the other party, the more they will be heard and accepted. The more they merely confirm the benefits you will obtain, the more likely they will be rejected and ignored.

Your opening offer should clearly state your interpretation of the issue, and your proposed solution: 'I would like to make an offer for the supply of product to your organisation. For the volume you are requesting, I can guarantee supply provided we have 40 days' notice and you can pick up from our warehouse. This would then allow us to offer a price of £150.00 per tonne.'

You can indicate the firmness of your offer by the use of language. The harder your language, and the stronger the tone of voice in which it is delivered, the firmer your offer will sound: for example, 'we would like . . .', 'we must have . . .', 'I am happy to discuss different options . . .', 'We cannot move from our bottom line, which is . . .'. How firm or how flexible you should make your opening offer will depend on your negotiation strategy – are you following a strategy 1, 2, 3 or 4 negotiation (see your planning guide from Chapter 5)? If you use differing communication patterns during the negotiation, then you will confuse the other party with your intentions.

This is only your opening position, so don't spend too long trying to persuade the other party to accept it. You need to hear their position, and then establish the gap you need to fill together. So ask the other party to put forward their initial thoughts and position.

Listen to and test positions

The second action in the positioning phase is to listen to and test the positions on offer. Once again, your negotiation strategic approach will guide you. A strategy 1 or 2 (good current relationship) will be more open and accepting. A strategy 3 or 4 (poor current relationship) is more sceptical and doubting and you are more likely to push back and question the other party's data, assumptions and conclusions to test the strength of their position.

At the same time your strategy will guide how you respond to questions and pressure from the other party on your opening position. If you are following a strategy 1 or 3 (build a better future relationship) then you have another opportunity to demonstrate your flexibility and your desire to accommodate the other party's needs in the way in which you respond to questions and demonstrate your listening.

However sceptical and firm your strategic approach, beware of taking a position that is too inflexible. A line in the sand should only be drawn if there is some element that is totally non-negotiable, perhaps on ethical or moral grounds. The danger with non-negotiable items is that they often become negotiable later in the discussions, and you not only have an embarrassing climb down but you have also indicated you are willing to compromise on your stated limits – so which other ones will you move on? I have been involved in a number of negotiations with trade unions where the company side has been adamant about 'cornerstones of the agreement which are not negotiable' only for them to be changed some months later with predictable consequences for the agreement and the reputation of the negotiating team.

Remember also that you are listening to, and testing positions. You are not trying to destroy the other person's arguments or persuade them that your case is better. You are in process style, which means you are using rational and logical arguments – but you are also open to rational response. You task is to understand the other party's opening position and gauge how firm or flexible they are. You are also indicating your willingness to discuss and how firm or flexible you are prepared to be. One of the dangers in negotiating is that you keep trying to persuade the other party of the benefits of your solution over theirs, and – as they are doing the same – both quickly end up in defensive and entrenched positions, where compromise is the only outcome possible.

Once the opening positions are on the table and tested for understanding and firmness, you are able to establish the gap between the two parties and assess how easy or difficult it will be to fill that gap.

You can then move on to the next phase in the OPEC sequence, which is exploring. This means changing communication style and behaviour, so, just like moving over the threshold between opening and positioning, check that the other party is also ready to move on, and signal the change in objective to them: 'If I can summarise our opening positions, your position is that you want xxxx, and my position is that I want yyyy. Is that how you see it? . . . So, we have established the gap between our positions, but we have also expressed a desire to get an agreement that suits us both in this negotiation. Is it OK with you if we move on and explore our thinking further and test out some options that might help make this happen? . . .'

Exploring phase

In the Exploring phase there are two key actions:

- Identify underlying needs
- Test exchanges.

This phase is all to do with deepening understanding, so the predominant communication style is people style. You need to listen empathetically to discover what is of real importance and interest to the other party, and also to share your underlying thoughts and interests, and then see what creative ideas both parties come up with that would fill the gap. This requires a degree of trust between the parties – a willingness to open up and discuss issues candidly, so your negotiation strategic approach will help to identify what you need to do, and how much effort will be required. Low trust will mean that sharing is not going to be easy for either party. Being prepared to take the risk of showing more trust to the other party in these situations is usually the best strategy. Trust builds trust, and showing that you are prepared to share first demonstrates that you are willing to take the risk.

If you have identified a negotiation strategy which is to build the relationship for the future, then you will want to spend more time in this phase, and put more effort into understanding the other party's motivations and interests. People style helps to build a relationship as it is a responsive style.

Identify underlying needs

There are two elements here – finding out the other party's underlying need and disclosing your own. By identifying the underlying needs or interests of the other party, you get a deeper insight into their motivations and uncover the potential for exchanges that will satisfy those needs. In order to uncover the other party's needs you must ask a lot of questions that probe for depth of understanding. These questions are in people style, so they are open questions and asked with genuine interest in finding out an answer and getting a deeper understanding. It is not an interrogation, nor an attempt to manipulate the other party by asking leading questions. It is listening with the intention of understanding.

A guiding technique for uncovering underlying needs was introduced in Chapter 5 – the five whys. You can use this tool to uncover your own underlying needs at the planning stage, or use it to guide your questioning of the other party during the negotiation. Using this tool in a dialogue needs some care so that it does not sound like a game or an interrogation, so vary the question, and make it clear that you are interested in uncovering the real drivers to the conflict, not trying to exploit the thinking of the other party by finding a weakness:

■ 'What does 'x' do for you?'

■ 'How does it help you?'

■ 'Why is this so important to you?'

■ 'I hear that this element is critical to you – can you tell me a little more about what is driving that for you?'

■ 'What is your interest here?'

■ 'I am really interested to find out what is really important to you'

■ 'What must you really have for this negotiation to be successful for you?'

■ 'What is your absolute bottom line requirement here?' and so on

Summarising and paraphrasing are essential parts of the effective use of people style. The fact that you have processed the words used does not mean that you have necessarily understood the total meaning, especially when it comes to expressing needs and interests which have an emotional connection. So, listening also means listening to the music and the dance of the communication. Really pay attention to the other person and listen for the meaning behind the words. This will give you clues for further probing.

The other party may not have any clear idea of what is important to them, or have done the sort of thinking involved in your planning about wants and needs, so they may not see the point of the questions or the reason for your interest in probing. So constant reassurance is a must, and your motive for the questioning should be obvious. The process is akin to a funnel (see Figure 6.3), where you start with broad and general information, then funnel the information by taking a line of questioning that probes deeper and deeper until you reach the nugget of insight. Then you might want to repeat the funnelling with another theme – especially if there seems to be more than one important need being expressed. Also use the funnel to check your assumptions and to make sure that you fully put yourself in the other party's shoes.

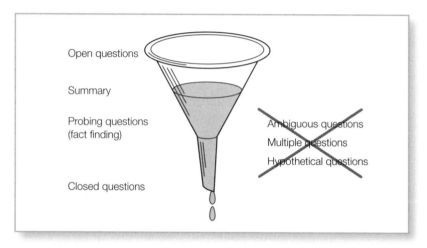

Open questions

Summary

Probing questions
(fact finding)

Closed questions

Ambiguous questions
Multiple questions
Hypothetical questions

figure 6.3   Question funnelling

Identifying underlying needs also requires you to disclose yours. Sharing your needs first helps to build rapport and trust – and opens the way to asking questions of the other party. You are demonstrating the sort of thing that you want to hear from them and further reinforcing your desire to work towards a solution.

If you feel that the other party is likely to withhold information and be less trusting (negotiation strategies 3 or 4), then you can disclose tactically by sharing your information a little at a time and seeking information from the other party in return: for example, 'Look, what's really important to me is to guarantee supply. I don't want to hold buffer stock unnecessarily. What is important to you in this deal?'

Test exchanges

In your planning, as well as thinking about what you want and need, you must also consider your haves. These are possible exchanges you can make with the other party that could satisfy their needs and therefore close the gap. You can ask the other party to offer you something that is of value to you that they haven't already mentioned, or you can offer something that you think might be of value to them that you haven't yet mentioned.

In either case, you should make the exchange offer conditional: 'What can you do for me so that I can give you X?', 'If I offered to include X, then could you give me Y?'. At no time do you want to make unconditional offers, as once you have ceded one you will come under increasing pressure to give another. The same applies to making concessions. Some negotiators feel that if they give a concession, then they are demonstrating good faith and it will help to build the relationship and lead to a settlement. In fact, making a concession unilaterally will indicate you are prepared to give up something for nothing, and will encourage the other party to push for more concessions and not give any themselves. If you need to make a concession, get something in return and make small ones.

The nirvana that you are seeking is to find exchanges that are of low, or no, cost to you but are of high value to the other party, and vice versa. That way, when each side totals up the value of the deal, they are both getting what they wanted, or in excess of that figure. You have win–win. The key focus here is on value not cost. Each party will have a different definition and understanding of cost and value, which is why you are testing exchanges in this action step. You have planned some ideas about what you have that the other party might find valuable, but you do not know the value that they place on these items until you test them out. Some items that you might think are valuable are not. Others which you think are worthless, are the most valuable.

For the same reasoning, the exploring phase needs to be conducted with an open mind which is always looking for options. This is where you can sometimes over-plan – you script the entire exchange, including what you and the other party will exchange, so that you then present these as a *fait accompli*, and do not listen to the other party. What you are doing is repositioning, not exploring. If you are truly listening, then you will hear new things, and these can spark off different creative thoughts in terms of what might be an exchange. Just as you don't need to offer the exchanges you planned, you don't need to restrict yourself to exchanges that you thought of earlier. As you uncover what is of importance to the other party, this will trigger new alternatives – or new questions, such as 'That sounds really important to you – what could I do to help?'

The most successful negotiators use more alternatives when putting together a deal, are more creative in their exchanges, listen more and react to emerging issues. This makes exploring the most critical phase of the negotiation. It is the phase when the most creative and long-lasting deals are made, and relationships are forged.

What should emerge from the exploring phase is a feeling that a deal is possible by combining a number of the exchanges discussed that seem to make a good deal for both parties.

Closing phase

In the final, closing phase there are two key actions:

■ Put a potential deal together

■ Make an agreement.

The key communication style for this phase is action, which has the outcome of a deal – the desired result of a negotiation.

Put a potential deal together

At its most simple, this step is a summary of the preceding step in exploring which pulls together the accepted exchanges that form the bargain:

> *'So, if I can summarise the discussion. You have agreed to deliver the goods to our locations within 14 days from order, and in return we will pay you the price of £XX per tonne, 50 per cent with the order and 50 per cent on delivery. Is that your understanding?'*

Of course, not all discussions will be that clear cut, but if the exploring phase has been well managed, there will be some possibilities that would form the basis of a deal. If the options are not clear, then it is a signal that you may need to explore some more or be prepared to return to exploring if your potential deal proposal does not work:

> *'I think we might have the basis of a deal. I can see that if I did X and also added in Y, and you were able to reduce your price by £Z, then that is something I could agree to. Do you see another potential deal?'*

This approach offers some final trading to close the gap and broker the deal. If you take this trading route, the requests should be small on both sides and, ideally, not on areas of principle that have not already been discussed. An expectation of a large final trade is more likely to extend the negotiation than close it, and suggests that the exploring phase was not completed effectively.

Another scenario in closing is that you or the other party, or both, need to consider the potential deal in more detail, get a final sign-off of the conditions, or seek authority to agree from another person in the organisation. Here, you should get a clear understanding of the summary deal, the next steps each party is making and a date for reconvening the discussion:

> *'So, the deal on the table is that you deliver the goods within 14 days from order, and in exchange we pay £XX per tonne, 50 per cent with the order and 50 per cent on delivery. We will adjourn the discussion so that we can confirm the details of the deal with our logistics and finance groups, and reconvene at 2pm on Wednesday to sign the agreement.'*

(Always fix a date and time and fix the conditions regarding who is doing what – don't leave it to chance or make an assumption that the other side sees things the same way.)

This is the step in the whole negotiating process that you have been leading up to, so, although you don't want to rush to get here and risk pushing for a deal too early, you equally don't want to put off closing the deal out. If the potential deal that you foresee doesn't fit, then it is quite likely that the other party is thinking about closure as well and has something in mind. It is important to ask for the deal. If it doesn't work, you can always retrace your steps into exploring. It is only a potential deal; all is not lost if it isn't immediately accepted. You just need to ask, 'What else needs to be there for the deal to work for you?' This then gives you the opportunity to push for what the salespeople call a 'presumptive close': 'If I agree to this condition, then we have a deal?'

Any sign of reluctance to close by either party might suggest that there are some lingering concerns or unexpressed fears about the negotiation. If one party is feeling uncomfortable at the end of a negotiation, this must be dealt with for the agreement to be successfully implemented. If it is not dealt with satisfactorily, then there is – at worst – a possibility that you won't get an agreement, and at best, there will be difficulties in implementing the deal. So, even though you are in action style, which is not responsive in its nature, you need to stay alert to the feelings and reactions of the other party.

Make an agreement

This is the final action step, and should reflect the understanding of the form of contract that was understood when discussing ground rules in the opening phase. It sends the wrong message of win–win cooperation if you suddenly spring a condition of agreement on the other party at the last minute. Your own, and the other party's, organisations might have some standard requirements for agreements and terms and conditions of contract. These are also potential areas for negotiation in their own right in more complex deals.

The simple requirement here is that there is an understanding and clarity on both sides about the agreement that has been reached. Even if you only need a verbal agreement it is always good practice to get it in writing, just so that there is a clear understanding on what has been agreed. Time spent just summarising the details will lead to much saved time in the future when managing implementation glitches.

Example

A negotiation using the OPEC model

Electec works in the electronics industry, specialising in the application of new technology to industrial measurement. It has four main departments, innovation, application, manufacturing and sales, with a small administrative and support centre:

- The innovation department is responsible for identifying new technologies for measurement, either from its own activity or through joint projects with university technology departments.

- The application department takes over the new ideas and ensures that they are commercially viable before putting together a business plan.

- The manufacturing department is responsible for in-house and contract production of the hardware and software.

- The sales department is the link between the customer and the company. Many of the ideas for new products come from salespeople who have identified a customer requirement.

The relationship between the departments is usually good, though they do work to different goals and performance measures. The innovation department prides itself on its creativity and its good working relationships with the university technology research departments. Some of the ideas are technically great, but are not economically viable, which is a fact of life, but the feeling is that the application department is often too cautious in its analysis and that industry leadership is lost through delay in getting new products into the marketplace.

Commercial viability is the basis of the application department's reputation. It prides itself on making sure that there is always value added to the company and that there are no expensive mistakes caused through lack of proper testing or evaluation of the technology. Too often, the innovation department delivers urgent projects with little testing and scant awareness of the commercial requirements of the business.

Pat, the Application Manager is about to meet with Johan, the Innovation Manager, about a new measurement device. The idea came from one of the sales engineers who had observed difficulties in creating the right mix of ingredients when visiting a customer site last year, and this new technology has been developed in a joint project with a university.

Johan wants a quick acceptance by application and to get the product into the market before the competitors. Pat is more cautious and wants to make sure it is a viable product, and already has a number of other technology trials underway. The university came up with a quick result, and the initial technical review is excellent. They both plan for the meeting.

Opening phase

Pat and Johan agreed to meet in a meeting room at the office rather than one of their own offices. This helped to set the climate as they were on 'neutral ground'; neither was risking being perceived as using position power. The atmosphere was friendly – they did have a generally good relationship – and they spent time reflecting on the common ground and successful discussions they had in the past. They agreed that it was most likely that this discussion would be equally positive and they could both see a successful outcome (*ideas style*). The timetable for the discussion was agreed and a simple verbal form of agreement was also agreed as being all that was required. When both parties felt comfortable that they were ready to proceed, by tacit agreement they moved into the positioning phase.

Positioning phase

As Johan was the party with most urgency, he stated his position first. They had a customer need, a new technology had been devised which worked well in initial trials, there were three competitors known to be working in the same area, so getting the system into production and into the market as soon as possible was essential for the company. He wanted to fast track the application process. A proposal for achieving this would be to put a beta version into the customer premises and do some of the testing on site so that they could get the publicity. He was willing to help out with supplying some engineering resource to the test as he knew that the application department was already stretched in testing and developing business cases for other products (*process style*).

Pat asked a few questions to check her understanding of the situation and the technology, then stated her position. Whilst she recognised that the initial results look promising, and there was a clear commercial opportunity in the industry, she must ensure that the project has viability before going public. The costs of a failure far outweighed the opportunities for an early advantage. With the late notice of this opportunity it had not been possible to plan evaluation trials into their schedule. There was insufficient funding to cover the costs of all products, so priorities must be set. In this case Pat estimated that testing would take about two months to complete, and it would be at least two more months before the current workload and the holiday season allowed a start (*process style*).

Johan tested and challenged some of Pat's arguments and reminded her that he had foreseen the staffing difficulty by offering some of his engineers to applications to help with the testing. Pat would not have to bear the burden of cost, just oversee the process. However, Pat reiterated that there was still a fundamental difficulty with releasing a product to the market that had not been properly evaluated, and all of the risks that were associated. They were beginning to reach an impasse. Despite amassing all of the arguments they could to persuade the other, little movement was taking place towards an agreement that satisfied both. Fearing that they would get stuck in a point–counterpoint discussion, Pat decided to move away from positioning.

Exploring phase

Pat recognised that Johan was fiercely defending his position and was trying to find every possible way to get this product into the market early. It was an interesting product, and it had some real potential in that there was at least one ready-made customer, but why was this product so important? Why the urgency? 'Johan, you seem particularly enthusiastic about this product and want to get it into the market quickly. I think I understand the commercial and technology leading future that you foresee for this product, but you don't always support cases with such vigour. So I am interested in why this product, and why now? What is driving this for you Johan?' (*People style*).

Recognising that Pat seemed really interested in understanding, Johan disclosed that he was under pressure from the Managing Director to cut costs – nothing unusual there – but this time he was looking to reduce the university funding. The MD saw this area as having few controls, little direction and poor performance.

What Pat heard was there was a potentially great product that had been developed by one of the university partnerships, and if this went into the market quickly, Johan would have some data to counter the MD's push to cut funding in this area. 'If that is the real need driving your wish to get this product fast-tracked, are you open to other suggestions that would keep the university funding that did not mean taking a risk on this product?' Johan said he would listen but could not see any other way. He was also interested to find out why Pat had been so adamant that even though he was offering to cover the cost of the application testing himself, she was still not willing to move her position. 'What is driving your reluctance to take up my offer?' (*People style*).

Pat explained that she and her department had been subject to a number of criticisms from the Board in recent months over the poor returns on some products. She could not afford to take another risk on a product – her own credibility and career was at stake. She needed time to consider developments in a calm atmosphere, not be pressurised into making a rush decision.

Johan could now see why Pat was so reluctant to release this product, and that his own behaviour in not involving her at the early stages of design could cause her to feel under more pressure in making decisions. He could see that if he brought Pat into discussions much earlier, it could help to protect her from what she saw as a great personal risk. He could build a number of Pat's concerns into the design at the initial stages.

It looked as though there was a potential for agreement that met each of their needs. Pat and Johan tested some potential exchanges. Johan saw that if he brought Pat in on new projects at the initial stages and built a close liaison with the application department to discuss early concerns, it would give Pat more time for evaluation. This would be of value to Pat, and at low cost to Johan.

In return, Pat recognised that Johan was under extreme pressure from the MD, and offered to have a meeting with the Board to support the case for continued university funding. She could show commercial successes that came from universities which would prove that they more than covered the cost. She was confident that the Board and the MD would agree when they saw the numbers. Once again, low cost but high value.

Closing phase

It was easy then to put together the deal. Pat summarised: 'I'll meet with the MD and the Board to get them to continue university funding, and in return, you will bring me in on new projects at the outset. Do we have an agreement? Great – now we have cleared up what really matters to us, let's talk about this new technology idea.' (*Action style*).

In the next chapter you will learn how to avoid some of the common pitfalls experienced by negotiators, learn from the experiences of successful negotiators and discover what to do when the going gets tough.

7

What successful negotiators do and don't do

This chapter draws from my own experiences of conducting and advising on negotiations in a vast range of situations and cultures from Europe to the USA to China to Russia, and from charities to SMEs to multinationals and to trade unions. I also draw on the research and writings of the experts in the field from whom I have learned my craft, and who have researched the psychology and practice of negotiation over a period of 40 years. These experts include Neil Rackham, the founder of Huthwaite International, who observed sales teams to discover what makes some people more successful than others, from which he developed the SPIN® sales technique; Chester Karrass who has written copiously on the subject and conducted laboratory exercises to identify behavioural conditions that make for greater success; Roger Fisher and William Ury of the Harvard Negotiation Project; Roger Harrison, David Berlew and Alex Moore of SMS, Inc. who developed a negotiation training programme based on these ideas which is recognised as one of the world leaders; Gavin Kennedy, Emeretus Professor at Heriot-Watt University in Edinburgh and author of several books on negotiation; and numerous clients, colleagues and workshop participants.

Common pitfalls

Lack of preparation

The most common mistake that negotiators make is not spending enough time preparing for the negotiation. Too many turn up at the meeting having had a quick look at the papers just beforehand,

and scribbling some notes on the back of an envelope. They have a mistaken belief that they cannot prepare or plan, because they don't know what the other party is going to say. All they can do is listen and react.

There is no excuse for not doing your homework and preparing for a negotiation, however small and insignificant. Even in the most extreme cases where you have absolutely no evidence or experience of the other party involved in the negotiation, it is still possible to do your research on their organisation, their business, the market and the environment, often without even leaving your own desk by searching all of the online resources that exist.

Doing homework and preparation pays off in manifold ways. Follow the guidelines and checklists in Chapters 5 and 6 to make sure that you prepare adequately.

Communication style preference

When you get into the interaction phase, there are a number of other common pitfalls, mostly to do with your own comfort in particular situations and with particular communication styles. Consider your own communication style preferences – you probably have one or two styles which are your 'go-to' styles: ones where you feel most comfortable, ones that you have used successfully in the past, ones that you like. There are other styles which you like less (or positively dislike) and find less comfortable to use or less successful. As all four communication styles are used in a successful negotiation, being good at a couple of styles means that you will be good at only half the negotiation!

A preference for process style (common in Northern Europe, large businesses, public sector organisations, and those based on technology or process management) will mean that you will be good at positioning, but also have a tendency to continue in logical persuasion for too long, ending up in a compromise outcome.

A preference for people style (common in those cultures and environments where relationship is seen as more important than task completion) means that you will spend a long time in opening, building a very successful relationship, and in exploring, looking for opportunities to satisfy the other party. You will probably be less firm in pursuing your own or your organisation's needs in the negotiation. This means a more accommodating outcome, weighted in the other party's favour.

An ideas style preference (common in start-up cultures and project-led environments where the future opportunity is most important) will deliver a great exploring phase, with masses of alternatives and ideas, but may fail to be grounded in the reality of what is feasible and possible to deliver. There is also an urgency to the ideas style which may push for a deal too quickly, at the first sign of an interesting opportunity.

Another style preference that will push for a premature deal is action (liked by the USA and Australia and other cultures where speed and outcome is of the essence, like sales, fast moving consumer goods and retail). The desire to get a deal means that there is a rush to closing, and the alternatives and opportunities will not be explored. Again, a tendency to leave with a compromise deal is the result.

To counter these personal tendencies, you can take one of three actions:

1 Develop your expertise in your weaker styles through practice, using some of the development exercises outlined in Chapter 10, or by following a communication skills training programme.[1]

2 Plan more carefully to complete the actions associated with the OPEC phases that are your less-favoured ones from a communication styles perspective.

3 Carry out your negotiations in a team where your weaknesses are balanced by another's strengths.

Not managing the OPEC phases

Often linked to your preference for the communication styles are pitfalls that are created by not following the action steps in the OPEC phases properly. As mentioned in Chapter 6, people usually do not spend enough time in the opening phase. The impact is that too little time is spent building positive relationships and climate for the negotiation, which then does not proceed on a good foundation. Our opening positions start to creep into the exchanges, and instead of making a clear distinction between the two phases and moving together, the other party could feel rushed and confused by the mixed messages you are sending.

The next pitfall is spending too long in the positioning phase, often linked with being comfortable with the process communication style. You are meant to be sharing the opening positions in this

[1] For details of books, exercises, courses and development activities in the four communication styles model used in this book, go to **www.gettingresultswithoutauthority.com**.

phase, not trying to persuade the other party of the merits of your solution or trying to argue against, or undermine, their opening position. An opening position is just that – an opening position. It is not the final position or solution, there are alternatives which can be looked at. So you don't move into exploring, with its change of focus and communication style.

Exploring involves listening, which you can't do effectively in process style. Process style is about data and rational argument in order to find a solution; it is not about suspending your judgement, listening for emotions and feelings and being tentative. In order to explore effectively you need to use people style and respond to emerging issues that you discover through empathetic listening. It is not about tabling prepared options and compromises in order to push for an outcome. These premature attempts to force a closure will build resistance from the other party who will be feeling steamrollered into an agreement. At the other end of the scale, staying too long in exploring and seeking a perfect solution is also counter-productive.

At the closing phase, other pitfalls emerge. One that is seen frequently in commercial negotiations is to seek a further concession at the point of signature, what the Americans call 'nickel and diming'. This practice of asking for something more – however insignificant – at the closure stage creates an annoyance in the other party. In some cultures it may be more acceptable, and even expected, so it may be something to protect yourself against, but it is never likely to be a positive strategy to use.

Another closing pitfall is to forget to forge a proper agreement and detail the implementation plan in the euphoria and celebration of reaching the deal. The dangers of making assumptions and not clarifying the detail at this stage are serious. The devil really is in the detail.

Taking advantage of the other party

It is very tempting to take advantage of the other party's mistakes or lack of skill in negotiating. The purpose of a negotiation is to get a deal, not smash the other party into the ground or make them pay for their errors. You are seeking a win–win outcome, so taking advantage – however it is done – is an inappropriate reaction, as it will almost certainly mean that your relationship with the other party will be lessened, certainly when they realise that they have been exploited.

Depending on the other party's skill at negotiation, you may need to put in a lot of effort to make sure that they get what they want. If they are not assertive, you may need to help them to put together a firm opening position. If they are not skilled in exploring alternatives, you may need to help them to listen. If they are not skilled in building relationships, you may need to help them here. In short, you may need to manage the negotiation from their side as well. The more you can ensure that the negotiation process and actions are completed, for both sides, the greater the chance of a win–win outcome.

If there is a perceived imbalance of power, giving the other party more power actually increases the success of the negotiation and avoids one-sided results which will be viewed as win–lose. According to research,[2] in situations where power is perceived to be equal, parties will share more information than would be the case in a relationship where there is a power imbalance. Pooling more information and resources creates a larger overall pie to be shared, making the opportunity of win–win more likely. Trying to position and push to show how much power you have in the negotiation is self-defeating. If the other party sees themselves as less powerful, then they will close up, share less information, and the parties will be less likely to create a bigger pie. I might get more of the pie, but it's more of a much smaller pie. A better strategy is to try to build the relative power of the other party, so that they feel equal and can create a larger pie to share.

Not having a pause button

Much of the content of the negotiation will emerge during the discussion – you will hear, probably for the first time, what the opening position of the other party is; you will hear what their needs are; you will hear some alternatives and ideas that you had not thought of; you will understand their motivations and interests – which is most likely different from the information you had to hand when you were planning. So to continue negotiating without considering this new information or perception is dangerous. But many negotiators feel the need to keep sitting there, trying to juggle the information in their heads and at the same time to continue to discuss things. They mistakenly feel either that they are capable of completing several different tasks simultaneously, or that taking a time out is a sign of weakness, or that they are not on top of the situation. So they don't hit the pause button.

The impact of this is that the information is not considered and analysed properly, significant data are missed or ignored and not acted upon. At best this leaves you agreeing to a deal which

2 Wolfe, Rebecca and McGinn, Kathleen (2005) 'Perceived Relative Power and its Influence on Negotiation', *Group Decisions and Negotiation*.

may not be the best on offer, and at worst aggravating your fellow negotiators by seemingly refusing to listen and act on important information that they have shared. You may also get 'locked in' by some of your own emotions and feelings that make you ineffective. For all of these reasons you may need to disengage from the discussion at some time in order to reconsider what has been said and to refocus and replan.

How to disengage?

It is good practice to think about how you will disengage at the planning stage. Consider, and practise, some approaches that are appropriate for the situation to hand. It may be as simple as calling a coffee break or suggesting a stretch or comfort break. In a more complex negotiation, it is perfectly reasonable for both parties to want to take some time out to consider all of the material on the table and think about a response, so suggesting that you do that – openly and transparently – is in the spirit of win–win negotiating:

> *'I really appreciate the amount of background information you have given on what you need, and the importance of the negotiation to you. It sheds a lot of new light on the issues that separate us and the opportunities to close the gap which is what we are trying to do. What I would appreciate now is a short break to consider all of this information and come back to you with a properly considered response. I am sure that you would also appreciate the opportunity to think about the information and data that we have been able to bring to the table. Shall we say 30 minutes?'*

It may also be politic or necessary to convene with your advisers or negotiating team to consider responses. This is particularly important if you need an external authority to proceed, or you need the agreement of your negotiating team. The latter need is prevalent in trade dispute and grievance negotiations where third parties and negotiation teams from both sides are used. In fact, in many of the really successful dispute negotiations, more time is spent outside the formal negotiating arena than inside. When you are away from the formal arena, it is possible to have a whole series of informal discussions and negotiations that allow you to test opinion and sound out the other party off the record, and out of the spotlight of the formal arena.

Having a pause button and a strategy to disengage from the negotiations, and to use it positively, is an asset to any negotiator.

What successful negotiators do more

Plan

The research evidence suggests that successful negotiators plan more, spend more time planning, focus more on the negotiation from the other party's perspective, and plan a wider range of possible alternatives and outcomes, than average negotiators.

Successful negotiators do more research on the other party, their business, their working environment and their motivations than average negotiators, and think more about issues, options and alternatives that they might raise. However, they do not just focus on the differences, they will direct three times as much attention on areas of common ground and pay more attention to the long-term implications of any deal.

When planning their positions and expectations for the negotiation, successful negotiators do two things: firstly, they will set their outcome objectives in terms of range of expectations with upper and lower limits rather than a fixed point; secondly, they will plan to deal with issues together or as separate discussions, not as a sequence. (Average negotiators tend to rely on a sequence of events: first I'll deal with X, which will lead to discussing Y, etc. This means less flexibility to respond to the other party's agenda, and being a slave to their plan.)

Finally, successful negotiators have and use their BATNA – the best alternative to a negotiated agreement – to build their power and allow them to have a clear and real alternative to avoid agreeing a bad deal.

Build the relationship

Successful negotiators spend longer building and put more emphasis on the relationship between the two parties, both during the negotiation and in their longer-term interests. They are themselves emotionally centred and are clear about their values, motivations and intentions. They have a collaboration mind-set first and foremost. They are comfortable sharing their own feelings and owning up to their own shortcomings and strengths in a way that is not condescending. Successful negotiators also make sure that any past resentments or misunderstandings are cleared up before trying to proceed with the current negotiation.

Successful negotiators have a more positive outlook than average negotiators, without being 'pie in the sky' – they use this to envision an image of the ideal outcome that attracts and inspires the other

party to engage fully in the negotiation. And they emphasise the similarities and common ground that exists with the other party, which
they have spent time researching at the planning stage.

Successful negotiators will also more frequently disclose propri-
etary data and information about their own feelings, underlying
motivations and needs in order to build trust and encourage a similar
disclosure from the other party (responsive/relationship focused communication). In contrast, average negotiators focus more on external
factors such as facts, clarification and general expressions of opinion
(non-responsive/task focused communication).

Get their message across clearly

Successful negotiators have planned their positions more effectively
than average negotiators and have more flexibility, but they will state
their position clearly and succinctly. When making a point, they
are willing to repeat it until the other person has properly heard it.
(According to some research, you may have to repeat something three
times to be properly heard and taken seriously, especially if the statement is something that the other party wishes to avoid.)

Successful negotiators also recognise that facts are not persuasive.
Average negotiators believe the more facts you pile up in order to
prove your point, the better. In fact, the other side becomes more confused. Successful negotiators limit their arguments to the two or three
strongest points.

The successful negotiator will also be more balanced in their message
delivery, offering both sides of an argument and discussing the pros
and cons (albeit emphasising the elements in their favour). Average
negotiators tend to get involved in more attack and defence cycles.
When successful negotiators disagree they first give the reasons for
their disagreement then state that they disagree, making the reasons
more likely to be listened to than if the sequence was reversed.

Successful negotiators also do not produce an immediate counterproposal in response to the other party's suggestions. They recognise
that the point at which a person is least receptive to another's idea is
if they have just presented one of their own. Successful negotiators
always consider and discuss the other side's suggestions before introducing any counterproposal. They wait until their proposal will be
received more favourably.

Reciprocate

Successful negotiators do not make unilateral concessions or unconditional offers. Both create the expectation of more concessions or offers without the other party having to do anything in return. Average negotiators often do make concessions and offers without any reciprocation in the mistaken belief that it is helping to build the relationship. Successful negotiators recognise the immense power of reciprocation in the human psyche, and make sure that as well as looking for exchanges, they will also respond positively to acts from the other party that demand a reciprocal response.

As well as looking for reciprocation in their deals, successful negotiators are also far more creative in their exchanges. They suggest more alternatives, are prepared to consider a greater range of alternatives and they ask more questions about alternatives than average negotiators.

Listen more and better

Successful negotiators test understanding and summarise more frequently than average negotiators. They reflect back what the other party has said to solicit a further response before themselves introducing any new ideas. Successful negotiators ask significantly more questions than average negotiators, and those questions follow the thinking of the other party and therefore do not feel like an interrogation.

Successful negotiators listen more for the feelings and meanings behind the words, are attuned to the music and dance of the other party, and will reflect that back to gain further insights into concerns and lack of understanding.

Mind their language

Successful negotiators avoid the use of words and phrases which can cause irritation, for example 'generous offer,' 'fair,' 'to be honest with you', and 'reasonable' to describe one's own statements and proposals. The impact is that you are suggesting that the other party is not being fair, generous and reasonable, or that you have not been honest so far. They therefore have an opposite effect to the intent. Huthwaite International's research found that skilled negotiators use 2.3 'irritators' per hour of face-to-face speaking time as compared with average negotiators who use 10.8. The average negotiator fails to recognise the counterproductive effect of using positive value judgements about themselves and, in doing so, implying negative judgements of the other party.[3]

Take more breaks

Effective negotiators take more breaks, recesses and time outs to consider the information given by the other party and to formulate their responses. They are also more proactive in offering the other party the opportunity to take a time out to consider their offers and information.

Review more

Successful negotiators review their negotiation process and outcomes more often, and spend more time reviewing, than average negotiators. (In labour disputes, trade union representatives typically review a negotiation more often, and in more detail, than the management representatives, which means they learn and hone their skills and strategies for future negotiations.)

Positive interaction

At a more general interaction level, we know from research, particularly that of psychologist Barbara Fredrickson and mathematician Marcel Losada that there is an optimum positive-to-negative interaction ratio in our work and personal life that leads to good relationships and improved performance.[4] If we look at marriage (an ultimate life negotiation for a long-term partnership agreement) it has been found possible to predict, with incredible accuracy, whether newlywed couples would stay together or divorce by observing and scoring their positive and negative interactions in one 15-minute conversation.[5] That research points to a positive-to-negative ratio of 5:1 as the 'magic formula'. Below that threshold, couples were most likely to divorce in the first few years. Above that threshold, they would stay married.

[3] Huthwaite International (2011) *Sales Negotiation Behaviours to Avoid*, Sales Tips Blog, **http://blog.huthwaite.com.au**.

[4] Fredrickson, Barbara and Losada, Marcel (2005) 'Positive affect and the complex dynamics of human flourishing', *American Psychologist*, vol. 60, pp. 678–86.

[5] Gottman, J. and Levenson, R. W. (2002) 'A Two-Factor Model for Predicting When a Couple Will Divorce: Exploratory Analyses Using 14-Year Longitudinal Data', *Family Process*, vol. 41(1), pp. 83–96.

Looking more widely at interpersonal relationships, the Fredrickson–Losada research points to a positive-to-negative ratio greater than 3:1 as a significant turning point in building relationships. Lower than 3:1 creates an unhealthy environment. At a 3:1 ratio working relationships become significantly more productive. Greater than 3:1 is fine, up to a top limit positive-to-negative ratio of 13:1. Above this level we lose sight of reality, as it seems that we need the contrast of negative to respond appropriately to the positive, otherwise we end up in the realm of blind optimism.

All of your interactions, however small, go to build up the positive-to-negative ratio and therefore build the positive climate you need for a successful negotiation. Acknowledging people, saying hello, showing interest, using encouraging words, stopping and listening to them, giving them full attention, giving positive feedback, saying thank you, responding quickly to them, asking for help and advice – all help in ensuring that you build a positive working relationship with the other party. Successful negotiators are more likely to use a positive-to-negative ratio of more than 3:1 in their interactions with the other party, no matter how deep the conflict. It is another example of separating the person from the issue – just because we have a serious dispute does not mean we have to be nasty to each other. In fact, being nasty is likely to produce worse outcomes.

Avoiding the pitfalls and following the practices of successful negotiators will help you to conduct better negotiations and also review and develop your skills and practice. In the next chapter, I focus on other things that might go wrong in a negotiation when the other party proves to be more difficult than predicted and does not 'play the game' by using tactics and 'dirty tricks'.

8

Tactics and dirty tricks – using them and dealing with them

Unfortunately, in the world of negotiation, not everyone plays to your rules. You may be following a strategy of win–win negotiating and see the potential for collaboration. The other party (or someone advising them) may come from a different school of negotiating and be looking to gain an advantage, or try to win, by any means. Some individual and organisation targets almost demand that negotiators show that they have achieved a significant result over the 'base case' they plan for in their objectives. This is particularly true of aggressive purchasing managers looking to reduce costs in the short term, or operations managers looking to prove that they are 'better' than purchasing in pursuing deals. Some parties will bring out dirty tricks to help them 'win' or perhaps to avoid reaching agreement. They aren't really dirty tricks, they are common negotiating tactics but they can feel like dirty tricks when they are done to you.

The objection to these ploys is not that all of them are always morally wrong or unethical, but that they tend to disrupt negotiations especially at the relationship level. No one can deny that they sometimes work and almost certainly you will use – or be seriously tempted to use – some of these tactics, consciously or unconsciously, because they are part of the negotiating arena. When you use them yourself, of course, they are not dirty tricks but a well thought out tactical strategy. However, the other party may not see them the same way.

Being caught out by tactics will leave you feeling in a losing position. Complaining about the use of unfair tactics is not likely to enhance the relationship with the other party. So what do you do when you feel the other party is resorting to dirty tricks? Awareness is critical, you need to be on your guard to recognise if a tactic is being used, and then you can choose what action to take. Doing nothing may be an option, and in many cases ignoring the tactic is the best option, but not always. In situations where you have to address the issue it is good to know that every tactic has a counter measure. So, in this chapter, I consider the common tactics used, how they manifest themselves, and how to deal with them in a positive way.

Lies

Lying in negotiations is common practice. Do you always tell the truth, the whole truth and nothing but the truth? Of course not – you are trying to put the information across in a way in which it benefits you, and the other party is doing the same. It is a matter of degree, ranging from sins of omission, through selective truth telling to never, ever, telling the truth on principle. Famously, Disraeli quoted that there are 'three kinds of lies: lies, damned lies, and statistics'. Figures can prove anything and 'facts' can be manipulated to suit the cause. Is this lying? Your answer to this question will depend on your values and whether or not you are on the receiving end.

When presenting facts everybody uses ones that suit their own position, and they will emphasise those points in their favour and play down (or ignore) the downsides. The salesperson wants to maximise the price, the buyer wants to lessen the price, and they will use tactics that help them to achieve that. Both sides need to be aware of this and act accordingly.

Countering

Check your assumptions and facts. Know the market. Always look for objective data not opinion, and if an opinion is proffered – 'Property in this area is selling at 20 per cent above the market at present' – and it is significant to the negotiation, this should prompt you to probe for the facts.

Confronting suspected liars directly is usually a bad idea and can often end relationships on the spot, particularly if the liar feels trapped in their own deceit. A better approach is to ask to recheck the figures, or ask to know on what assumptions they are based: 'My market data seems to be different to yours. I am only seeing a 10 per cent premium. Can we pool our sources?'

Lacking authority

A common delaying tactic is to claim limited authority in the hope that you will settle for what is on offer rather than wait for higher authority to be sought: 'Your proposal is interesting but I will have to take it back to my boss for final approval.'

Countering

Check out who has the authority to agree in the opening phase, and if necessary negotiate with the other party to have that person present in the negotiation so that an agreement can be reached.

However, it is particularly important when negotiating internationally to recognise that there are some cultures where you can only speak to someone of the same status as yourself. So, if the decision maker is of higher status, then you would need to bring someone in from your side of similar status to ensure they can be present. To do otherwise would be seen to be rude and a loss of face. (See the next chapter for more information on international and cross-cultural considerations in negotiations.)

Deadlines and deadlocks

These tactics can be used to positively bring a negotiation to a close, or to exert pressure on the other party to offer concessions – especially when the deal is highly important for the other party. Interestingly, a deadline imposed by one party is often accepted without challenge – 'We need to complete the deal by 5pm on Friday' – whereas it is more often than not an arbitrary limit that is not particularly significant.

The threat of a deadlock puts pressure on the negotiator to agree to something or go home empty handed and with a sense of failure (especially if your management have told you to not come back unless you have a contract, and you have taken an expensive trip in both time and money!).

Countering

Always remember that having no deal is better than agreeing to a bad deal. Bad deals are lose–win, so the relationship is lessened, and there will be resentment leading to difficulties in implementing this deal and in negotiating any future deals. It is usually better to come back empty handed from a negotiating trip and explain the circumstances to your boss, than to commit your organisation to a deal that is not in the organisation's interests.

A well worked-out and effective BATNA (see Chapter 5) will add strength to your negotiating position and give you a powerful defence to deadline and deadlock pressure. Having a valid fall-back position means that you do not need to conclude this deal.

In reality, deadlines and deadlocks are nearly always negotiable. Raise it with the other party and determine why it is important. If it is important and you can agree to it, then seek a concession from them as well: 'I can agree to your deadline of 5pm on Friday so long as we can make the first delivery by the end of this month.' Never make a concession under pressure without gaining a concession from the other party. If you cannot accept it, then raise it as an issue and discuss the ramifications of the threat.

Exploiting distance

Deadline and deadlock pressure is especially powerful when one party is well away from their home base. Apocryphal stories abound of negotiators from the USA (where quick deals are the norm and relationships are not important) going to Japan (where relationship building is the norm and a deal cannot be done without it) and finding themselves under extreme pressure to agree a deal when they are in the taxi to the airport to get their return flight. The time they had allocated to talking business and negotiating had been taken up with introductions, entertaining, social activity and – in their eyes – deliberate avoidance of discussing the business. This may, or may not, have been a deliberate tactic by Japanese negotiators to gain an advantage, but it is certainly true that some negotiators will try to exploit distance and jet lag to gain an advantage.

Countering

If you are travelling internationally in order to negotiate, make sure you leave yourself enough time to recover from any jet lag, and leave enough time for the negotiations so that you are not under pressure to get your return flight. In some cultures, especially those with high status norms and consensus decision making, negotiations are much more formal and drawn out, with frequent pauses for consultation with the negotiating partners and senior managers. If there are local customs that include lavish entertaining, then again, leave yourself enough time and space to deal with these (and time to recover!). Know your local customs by doing your preparation well, and be prepared for anything out of the ordinary.

Nibbling

This is a common tactic in sales negotiations. Just at the point of closing the deal, the negotiator asks for further small concessions: 'I think we're very close to a deal if we can just agree on this last item.' The danger is that if you give way on this concession you will most likely be asked for another. The negotiator nibbles away at your side of the deal.

Countering

Once again, the rule is to never give a concession without getting something in return. If you can give the concession, then trade for it. If you can't give the concession, say so and refuse. It is also an opportunity to use a presumptive close: 'So, you'll sign the contract if we agree to this?'

Stressful environment

Places that are difficult and hard for you to get to; not being offered food or drinks; being kept waiting without any apology or explanation; uncomfortable seating; looking into a glare or strong light. These are all signs that the other party might be trying to gain an advantage by putting you under stress.

Countering

Of course, it might not be a tactic or dirty trick – it may just be that the other party has innocently put you in this position. Treating it as an innocent mistake in your mind means that you don't attribute malicious tactics to the other party and blurt out a negative comment. So, identify what is happening to you, and if you can live with it, then ignore it and you will not be under stress, whether intended or not. If you can't live with it, then politely ask for what you want: 'Could I have a glass of water, please?', 'Would it be alright to draw the blinds, the sun is in my eyes'. Alternatively, move your chair or ask for a time out in order to regain your composure.

Unreasonable demands and offers

Understanding someone's offer or demand is not the same as accepting it. You should seek to understand the other party's offers and demands, but once they are on the table, they gain validity – unless you challenge them. This tactic may reveal itself in what the

Americans call 'high-balling' or 'low-balling' – the negotiator starts with an extremely high or low offer. The hope is that this will affect the bargaining range in their favour.

Countering

Always question and challenge so that you do not leave an unreasonable or outrageous offer or demand 'on the table'. Knowing what is 'unreasonable' or 'outrageous' is another reason for doing your preparation well so that you know the market. You can then use the same counter as for lying: 'My information seems to be different to yours . . . Can we check our assumptions and sources?'

Good guy/bad guy

One person plays the good guy, trying to be accommodating and keeping the negotiation moving; another person plays the bad guy, attacking and imposing limits and barriers. The hope is that the good guy can get more concessions in return for managing the bad guy.

Countering

This is another situation where you need to identify the tactic and discuss it: 'It seems that there is some disagreement on your side, would you like a recess to clarify your position?'

Threats

'If you don't agree to our demands by Friday, we will go on strike.' They may be bluffing, or the threat may be real. Either way, it is an indication that the other party wants to put a great deal of pressure into the situation; they are playing a high stakes game of 'take it or leave it'.

Countering

Raise the threat as an issue and discuss the ramifications of allowing it to stand. If it is a bluff, then you are calling it. If it is a real threat, then it becomes the subject of the negotiation: 'We cannot negotiate under threat. Can we discuss why you feel that it is appropriate to issue this ultimatum? What is driving your need?'

Threats can also be countered by small attacks that undermine the other party's commitment to the threat – sometimes referred to as 'salami slicing'. If they demand a meeting by the 10th, offer one on the 11th.

Scrambled eggs

In this tactic, the negotiator deliberately makes a deal complex to create confusion, for example by using lengthy and jargon-filled legal contracts or conditions of sale. There is always a danger that there is some clause that is heavily in their favour which they hope you do not notice.

Countering

Never sign anything without reading it thoroughly, and never agree to something you don't understand. If necessary, call a time out so that you can take your time to understand the details, and ask for any confusing items to be explained. Sometimes the need for such detailed contracts suddenly disappears.

General comments on tactics

▪ A tactic that is deployed to manipulate becomes impotent when it is identified. The intention is to change your perception and expectation in favour of the other party. If you recognise what is happening, then your perception and expectation is not affected.

▪ Watch your language. In identifying and 'calling' the behaviours involved here it is very easy to sound sanctimonious. At the least it is easy to start using language like 'fair', 'reasonable', 'ethical' to describe your behaviour, and by implication suggest the other party is being unfair, unreasonable and unethical. This, whether intended or not, is likely to deepen the problem and make it less likely that you can get a relationship-saving outcome.

▪ Separate the person from the problem. You are not in the negotiation to change the behaviour or values of the other party. Focus on the outcome and exchanges that get the outcome that each party needs.

▪ Be courteous: 'Nobody ever got a worse deal by being courteous.'[1]

---

[1] Kennedy, Gavin (2004) *Essential Negotiation: An A-Z Guide,* London, The Economist/Profile Books.

■ Prepare, prepare, prepare.

- Do your homework at the preparation phase – know the environment, know the other party, know the cultures at play.

- Prepare your defence mechanisms – know your BATNA, know your market, know your limits.

- Prepare your responses – practise identifying and negotiating the common tactics, rehearse your response to ones you might expect from your preparation, prepare your time-out strategies.

Negotiating in more complex situations

Although the general formulas and approaches outlined in this book are applicable to all situations where a win–win outcome is desired, some negotiations are more tricky than others. In many cases, the complexity is brought about by the scale and size of the issue to be negotiated. It then becomes like the relationship between project management and programme management – there are a number of different, interlinked negotiations taking place that need to be managed in a coordinated programme to reach the desired outcome. In the case of major partnership deals and organisation mergers, these negotiations involve possibly hundreds of people and a very lengthy period of time. But each negotiation is a relatively simple affair that follows the formula for a successful outcome outlined in the foregoing chapters. It is just the scale that makes for the complexity.

In other situations, the introduction of other factors make for the complexity. In the previous chapter, I looked at times when the other party may not appear to be following the same rules as you. This makes getting to a win–win outcome more difficult and complex. It could be that the other party has a very low perception of their power, and is inexperienced in negotiation. This means that you have to put a lot of effort into managing the negotiation, building their own power balance perception and stopping yourself taking undue advantage from the situation. In other situations, which is the subject matter of this chapter, there are other pressures or considerations which make the negotiation more difficult. The need to take into account the different cultures of the parties in, for instance, international negotiations; the need to manage the relationships with a negotiating team on your own side; the need to conduct negotiations remotely over the internet or telephone. All of these factors add to the complexity of planning and conducting the negotiation.

International and cross-cultural negotiation

The story in Chapter 2 of the Swedish and French car manufacturers' inability to conclude a deal due, in no small part, to the differences of culture between the two sides, shows the vital importance of understanding and preparing to encounter different cultures in the negotiating arena. Not all differences are as significant or as harmful as this story demonstrates, but even small differences can derail a negotiation, and at best can cause a lack of understanding on either side which can build into resentment or conflict.

From my own experiences of inter-cultural conflict, the root of the dispute is often the belief that what is 'right' or 'polite' as defined by my own cultural values is often perceived as 'wrong' or 'rude' in the other culture's values. So without meaning to we cause offence. And when differences are identified, people tend to judge them on moral grounds: that the other culture's standards are lower than yours, or that the other party has bad intentions, that they are being deliberately difficult, rather than attributing the behaviour to adherance to a different set of rules.

Cultural differences are not exclusive to international encounters. A culture is, after all, just a set of shared attitudes, values, goals and practices that characterises a group. Cross-gender, cross-generational, cross-functional, cross-racial, cross-religious, cross-class and cross-company situations are just as likely to show up cultural differences that get in the way of effective dialogue. In fact, these differences often hit hardest as people tend to prepare less for their eventuality. You think about the differences when you go to another country and expect another language. These show up as obvious differences. You tend to think less about the differences in your own everyday environment where cultural differences may not be so obvious.

Factors influencing cultural difference

When you are preparing for a negotiation with people from another culture, whatever that culture may be, the starting point is doing some careful preparation and research. Find out all you can about the culture, concentrating on actual experiences rather than theory. When you are researching, think about the situation you will be in and look for comparable data. For example, much of the writing on different

cultures is about how to live in that culture and the general characteristics of the people in that culture. In conducting a negotiation with
that culture, you will not be living there, just visiting, and the people
that you are dealing with will, in all probability, not be typical.

However, it is useful to consider some of the fundamental differences
between cultures in order to start to understand some of the more
subtle differences that exist, whilst avoiding the trap of stereotyping.
Many writers have formulated some general rules that differentiate
culture which help us to understand difference. These are the frames
of reference that the culture uses to engage with the world. Geerd
Hofstede's model[1] itemises five dimensions.

Hofstede's five dimensions

1 **Power distance**: the degree to which it is acceptable that some
   in society are more equal than others: for example Scandinavian
   countries tend to be more egalitarian and consultative, giving
   weight to all opinions and delegating decisions; China, Russia,
   Malaysia and India tend to be more stratified and autocratic,
   decision making is strongly centralised around hierarchy, age
   and status.

   When dealing with these latter, high-power distance cultures, you
   need to acknowledge a leader's power and be aware that you
   may need to go to the top for answers and decisions. In
   low-power distance cultures, be prepared to involve more people
   in the decision making and promote team working.

2 **Individualism or collectivism**: a continuum of responsibility from
   taking care of yourself to loyalty to an in-group. The American
   and European countries tend to be more individualistic, where the
   task comes before the relationship and decisions are speedy;
   Asian and Arab countries tend to be more collectivist, where the
   relationship is more important than the task and decisions take
   time and consultation.

---

[1] Hofstede, Geerd (1991) *Cultures and Organisations*, London, McGraw-Hill
   International.

In more collectivist cultures, show respect for age and wisdom, respect traditions and introduce change slowly. In more individualist cultures, acknowledge accomplishments, don't ask for too much personal information and encourage debate and expression of ideas.

3 **Masculinity or femininity**: the degree to which society sticks with and values traditional gender roles (men are tough, assertive, concerned with material success; women are modest, tender, concerned with quality of life). The masculine countries (preserving the traditional roles) are Japan, China, the USA and some European countries such as the UK and Germany, where decisiveness, assertiveness and performance are valued; feminine countries (traditional roles do not exist) are other European nations such as the Netherlands and the Scandinavian countries, where intuition, consensus and harmony are valued.

When working with a masculine culture, be aware that people may expect male and female roles to be distinct, so men avoid discussing emotions or making emotionally-based decisions or arguments, and should be seen to be leading. For feminine cultures, avoid gender stereotypes, and ensure equal male and female representation.

4 **Uncertainty avoidance**: how much you feel threatened by the unknown or uncertain situations. Less anxious cultures (low-uncertainty avoidance) like Singapore, China and the UK tend to be more relaxed, take account of all opinions and value the content of the decision; more anxious cultures (high-uncertainty avoidance) like Latin European countries (Greece, France, Belgium, Spain) and Latin American countries, Germany, Japan and South Korea tend to have strict laws and rules, take account of the opinions of experts, and value the process of decision making.

In high-uncertainty avoidance cultures, you need to be clear and concise, plan and prepare, communicate often and early, and provide detailed plans and limited choices. In low-uncertainty avoidance cultures, limit your use of rules and unnecessary structure, be calm and express curiosity when you discover differences.

▶

5 **Long-term orientation**: this dimension refers to how much
   society values long-standing – as opposed to short-term –
   traditions and values. This fifth dimension was added in the
   1990s to reflect the strong difference between Asian countries
   with their strong link to Confucian philosophy and Western
   cultures. In countries with a high, long-term orientation – the
   Asian countries – delivering on social obligations and avoiding
   'loss of face' are considered very important. More short-term
   orientation cultures – the USA and Europe – are more focused on
   equality, individualism and immediate results.

   So, when dealing with Asian countries, you need to show
   respect for traditions, not display extravagance or act frivolously,
   reward perseverance, loyalty and commitment, and avoid – at
   all costs – doing anything that would cause another to 'lose
   face'. (This also includes doing anything where you put yourself
   in a position where you could 'lose face' as the other party
   would be compelled to help you to 'save face'. Hence the
   problem of asking a direct question – the other party cannot
   answer ''no' as that would put them in a position where you
   would lose face. They will evade the question or give a
   non-committal answer instead.)

Using the Hofstede model, or any other similar model, you can prepare for your cultural encounter by identifying the key differences
between your own culture and the other party's. It will give you a
general sense of what is different. By adding this analysis to other
information about the typical behaviour of negotiators, you can create
a checklist of the different negotiating characteristics of the cultures
you work with.

Don't stereotype/don't mimic

First of all, recognise that there are a lot of sub-cultures. People living
and working in Europe often express incredulity when an American
talks about a single European culture. Yet it is all too easy to fall into
the same trap and talk about Asian cultures or Arab cultures as if
they are all the same. There are some similarities, but the differences
between Japan, China, Korea and Vietnam are enormous. And in
China, the regional differences are great, as are cultural differences

between the industrialised urban areas and the rural farming communities. So make sure that you research the right sub-culture as well as the national culture and don't use too broad a definition.

Then, once you have a clear understanding of the culture and sub-culture, question it unmercifully in the light of the individual(s) who form the negotiating team for the other side. Do not believe that everyone in the culture will behave the same way. I have encountered, amongst others, informal Germans, direct Japanese, logical Italians, quiet Spaniards, confronting Chinese, status-conscious Scandinavians, multi-tasking Swiss, impatient Irish and Americans who are not time conscious. To stereotype is dangerous.

Win–win negotiation is built on trust and the development of an ongoing relationship. Understanding the important factors of another's culture is a sign of respect, a way to build trust and credibility, and an indication to the other party that you want to build a relationship. Holding assumptions and stereotypes of another's culture generates distrust and builds barriers to building relationships and credibility. You need to be reserved and cautious and treat everyone as an individual. What are the important factors for them? How do they see the differences? How do they want to progress? How can you both build a greater understanding of each other to help build trust and relationships? These are all elements for the opening phase of OPEC, and suggest that in cross-cultural situations you should plan to spend longer and put more effort in this phase. Certainly when dealing with cultures where relationship is seen as more important, you probably cannot spend too long here.

Remember also that you come as a representative of your own culture. The purpose of preparing and knowing about the other culture is not to adopt it completely and mimic the other party. Mimicking is disrespectful and will also generate distrust and lower credibility. It is important to be polite in the other's culture, but it is equally important to be yourself. When receiving visitors from another culture, it is expected that they follow the basic rules of courtesy and politeness, but it is also expected that they be themselves. In another culture you are not trying to be the other person – you are yourself, being respectful. Know and understand the rules of politeness in the society so that you do not, inadvertently, make a *faux pas*. Very often the rules of politeness and friendship in one culture are rude and offensive in another: for example a Spaniard should not greet an Arab woman by kissing her on the cheeks; an American should not take a Japanese business card, write on it and then stuff it in his pocket. These basic rules of courtesy are the same as you would expect from people from another culture visiting you.

International culture – a third way?

As the business world becomes even more global, you can also see the emergence of a 'third culture' of the international negotiator. The differences between the national cultures have merged into a generally accepted business approach, often adopting more of the Western model as the norm for international business discussions. Whilst this may facilitate understanding and agreements at one level, it also poses its own problems.

The 'real' cultural values of the other party might exist but be suppressed. For example a negotiator from China has worked in the USA and has an MBA from a top university, and has learned and adopted a more 'Western' way of doing things based on results and outcomes. But when it comes to engaging in a negotiation that really matters to them, they might find out that their true values of face and *guanxi* start to surface. (In China the notion of *guanxi* is the basis of social and business activities in China, and consists of personal connections and relationships defined by reciprocity, trust and mutual obligations that goes way beyond Western concepts of networking. Chinese business people cultivate an intricate web of *guanxi* relationships, which may expand in a huge number of directions, and involve lifelong relationships. Reciprocal favours are the key factor to maintaining one's *guanxi* web, with failure to reciprocate being considered an unforgivable offence. This can lead to what Western cultures would see as corruption and nepotism.) The Chinese negotiator is unsettled and unhappy fighting an internal battle of values, and the other party is confronted with unexpected behaviour. It is always, therefore, appropriate to listen very carefully to the signals (not just verbal) from the other party to make sure that your assumptions on relationship and culture remain valid throughout the negotiation.

Another danger of the emergence of an international culture is that you might conclude a deal which works with the prime negotiator, only to find that implementation is not that easy when a more local, traditional culture emerges.

Example

This example is from my own consulting experience. A major multinational energy company based in the UK found that its agreement to offshore a great deal of its financial back office operation to India was fraught with problems between the UK managers and managers in India. When negotiating the deal with the

Indian company – one of the largest operations of its type in India – the details of how the arrangement would work, where responsibilities lay, quality standards on accuracy and timing, and communication processes were all agreed. Cultural differences were taken into account and built in to the processes and procedures. Systems were designed and tested to support the detailed agreement. These were piloted in the UK with a team of managers from the Indian company working with the UK managers who would be overseeing the operation to test and check the systems and processes. All worked well, and a number of changes were made to improve the processes.

When the system went live in India, problems started to emerge. The processes did not work as well as in the pilot, communications started to break down, responses from India were not as expected, accuracy and timeliness of data started to decline. On the surface, there was no difference from the pilot operation, when everything was live in the UK to the actual operation in India. The difference was tracked down to cultural differences between the managers who negotiated the deal and conducted the pilot on behalf of the Indian company, and the managers who operated the process in India. On the surface they were the same – they had the same education, the same level of qualifications, came from the same culture, had experience of the same type of work, were the same age and gender mix … The difference was that the negotiators and the managers who ran the pilot operation were used to the international environment – they had negotiated and set up a number of similar operations across Europe and the rest of the world, they had adapted to the more Western way of doing things and communicating. The local managers in India had not had the same exposure to the international circuit and behaved in a more traditional way. Despite the company doing its best to be culturally sensitive in its set up, it was caught out by not recognising that there were different sub-cultures at work in its partner organisation.

Using the cultural differences

Culture affects who you are and who the other person is. So when planning, consider what differences might be significant. Culture affects both what you want and how much you want. The other party's culture will affect what they want. Culture affects your priorities and the other party's priorities.

Wants, needs and haves are strongly affected by cultural background. The physical and the psychological distance between you and the other party may make it difficult to anticipate the other's wants, needs and haves, especially those culturally sensitive and more psychological wants, needs and haves that do not directly relate to the main issue of the negotiation. This area of planning demands research and creativity, best done with the assistance of someone who knows the culture you are going to.

The power balance in the negotiation is affected by a number of factors which contrive to put more pressure on the traveller, and therefore lower the feeling of power. The issue for negotiation will generally be more significant than a local issue; competition comes from more sides, you are away from your home dealing with jetlag, different climate, food, and possibly unknown situations, it is harder to get support from your home base, your bosses may expect more from you, and there is extra stress in having to deal with differences in behaviours, attitudes, customs and etiquette. To overcome the lowering effect on your power, extensive physical and psychological preparation, developing your international negotiating skills and detailed planning for the negotiation before you step onto the plane, will tip the power balance back in your favour.

Negotiation is seen differently in different countries. Some tactics that you see as 'dirty tricks' are often part of the general fabric of a negotiation in other cultures. A 'take it or leave it' approach is very well accepted in some cultures as a part of negotiation rather than the last option meaning that it has in Western cultures. Haggling over each and every item is an art form in some cultures, without any concern about the time it takes (wastes?). So when planning a negotiation strategy you will need to consider the cultural differences and how you will therefore plan to conduct the negotiation.

Finally, don't forget to consider all of the cultural differences at play. There is not just nationality, there is language, religion, education, gender, sexuality, race, class, experience, expertise, all of which go to make up the individual cultural mix of the person you are negotiating with. Some of these areas will be significant to you. Some may be significant to the other party. Some will be insignificant to you both. In your planning you need to take note of all the potential differences. In your interaction, you need to listen and check your assumptions and planning with the reality of what is before you.

Negotiating remotely

Negotiating on the telephone

Using the telephone is generally far less satisfying than communicating face-to-face. You are deprived of the expressions and body language of the people with whom you are negotiating, and of the closeness of contact that builds rapport and relationships. Yet using the telephone, telephone conferencing and video conferencing is fast becoming a norm for business as it becomes more global in its reach, more immediate in its decision making, and as communications technology improves. 'Is it worth the time and expense to travel around the world to attend a meeting?' is a question heard across businesses on a daily basis. And, according to recent research from INSEAD and the Kellogg School of Management at Northwestern University,[2] the quality of the negotiation may be unimpaired by not being face-to-face. What is important is the nature of existing (or non-existing) relationships.

The researchers found that when unacquainted individuals enter into a negotiation or group decision-making situation, the use of richer communication channels – face-to-face and video conferencing – allows people to see and hear each other, helps to establish rapport and increases the likelihood of achieving high-quality outcomes. Non-verbal cues such as tone of voice, facial expression and gestures allow these communicators to learn more about the other side and potentially trust them enough to share and integrate information. The researchers also found that richer channels contribute to higher-quality outcomes in larger groups and more complex tasks.

The researchers also discovered that when negotiators share a pre-existing relationship that fosters a cooperative attitude they think the best of their partners and communication is interpreted with the best of intentions and inherent levels of trust. As a result, face-to-face

---

[2]   Swaab, Roderick, Diermeier, Daniel, Galinksy, Adam and Medvec, Victoria (2012) 'The Communication Orientation Model: Explaining the Diverse Effects of Sight, Sound and Synchronicity on Negotiation and Group Decision-Making Outcomes, *Personality and Social Psychology Review*, Vol. 16, No 1, pp. 25–53.

interaction becomes less important for sharing information and nego-tiating and people can easily reach mutually beneficial agreements through virtual interactions.

Cultural background also affects the use and effectiveness of remote communication channels. People from a more collectivist culture (Eastern values) tend to approach a conversation with a more coop-erative orientation, and as a result may be less strongly affected by the communication channel used. For individualist cultures such as those in the West, however, negotiators have more independent or neutral orientations and need the richer communication channels of face-to-face and video conferencing to achieve high-quality outcomes.

When using the telephone for negotiating, you should – as for all negotiations – be well-prepared. And the use of the telephone means that it is easier to have your notes and preparation to hand to refer to during the negotiation. It is much easier, and less embarrassing, to shuffle the papers on your desk than in a face-to-face meeting. Unless it is a video conference, the other party cannot see what you are refer-ring to, so you can afford to have your research information to hand.

As part of your physical preparation, invest in a headset – it can be very tiring to hold a telephone receiver to your ear for a long period of time, and using a loudspeaker is distracting to the other party as it amplifies all of the ambient noise, creates a delay in the transmission, reduces sound quality and creates the possibility of echo and feedback. Also with a headset, you can move around (sometimes useful to help your thinking) and gather the information on your desktop.

When negotiating remotely in the interaction phase, bear in mind that as you are missing the non-verbal clues, the potential for misun-derstanding the other party is increased enormously. So listen more attentively, summarise and check understanding more frequently than you would do in a face-to-face conversation. Also remember that in a telephone conversation it takes up to five times the amount of time and effort to build rapport and a working relationship as it does in a face-to-face environment. Unfortunately, even though people and organisations may know this, they tend to spend less time in the open-ing phase and building a relationship when talking remotely: 'OK, everyone is online, so let's get down to business . . .'

To be even more influential on the telephone, exaggerate your voice tone. The focus of attention is entirely on the voice, so you can get your message across better if you concentrate on the voice tone. One easy way to do this is to exaggerate the dance of the style – if you want to sound assertive, stand up; if you want to sound pleased, smile; if you want to listen, lean forward and take up an open position.

With all forms of immediate communication like email and tel-ephone, there is a sense of immediacy and the need for instant responses. So be aware that you might be tempted into making fast, unwise decisions. There is nothing wrong in taking a time out: 'Let me give that idea some serious consideration – I will call you back in 10 minutes.' This gives you time to consider what is being said in a calm, reflective way and gives you time to plan to make the appropriate response. But don't forget to return the call or email at the time you promised, or you lose trust and credibility in the eyes of the other party.

Negotiating by email

When negotiating via email and instant messaging the research findings referred to earlier also stand: a pre-existing relationship giving a basis of trust between two negotiators protects the interaction against a potential spiral of misinterpretation and mistrust. Misinterpretation can occur more easily than with telephone communication as the receiver is totally dependent on the words alone for the meaning of the message. Hence the use of 'smileys' to indicate subtlety of message in an email. If the two parties have a history of communication, they know each other and are less likely to misinterpret.

Face-to-face business interaction contains over three times the volume of information as a typical business email communication exchange, and observations show negotiators communicating via email being less 'in sync' with one another, as judged by the amount of subject switching in the exchanges. It has also been observed that email negotiators ask 10 times fewer clarifying questions than face-to-face negotiators.

Skilled email negotiators benefit from some other properties of email, such as the fact that it gives people more time to think before reacting. In a face-to-face negotiation there is often a time pressure that delivers hastily constructed, less than optimal settlements. Email makes slowing down and considering responses easier.

However, even though email communication is more efficient in some areas, what is clearly missing in most business email communication is the non-business element. To help in building rapport and relationship, especially where there is no pre-existing relationship, bringing these personal, rapport-building elements into the opening phase of the negotiation by exchanging pictures, background information or personal phone calls before launching into an email negotiation will significantly improve the outcome. A negotiation is an exchange between two people, and the more they respect, understand and relate to each other, the better the negotiation outcome. So the exchange of social and emotional information is just as important as the exchange of hard facts. A mix of email with voice and video communication may be the best balance.

Research into email negotiations shows that when no prior relationship existed between negotiators, then negotiations were more likely to end in a deadlock or no result. Mutual sharing of personal information and focusing on building a relationship creates a higher likelihood of a successful negotiation.[3]

Other research identifies that email negotiations accentuate some areas, not always positively. Some behaviours that work in face-to-face negotiations may backfire in email negotiations. For example, making multiple-issue exchanges is a critical element of exploring and achieving win–win outcomes – they create a bigger cake. Email negotiators are observed to make more multiple-issue offers than face-to-face negotiators, yet this behaviour did not effectively expand the cake. The value did not seem to be as obvious to the parties. So, behaviours that have beneficial effects in face-to-face contexts don't appear to have the same impact in an impoverished communication medium. And, behaviours that may hinder negotiations in face-to-face contexts (e.g. threats and ultimatums) seem to be even more disastrous when used on email.

Once again, success in email communication is down to good preparation, listening attentively and considering the other party when sending and reading the exchanges. It is a fast and immediate communication medium, but it also allows you to slow down and consider your responses before hitting the send button. It is a good discipline to use the slow pedal when communicating by email.

Negotiating on the internet

Moving further away from personal contact in negotiation is by purely using online applications on the internet. Most of these applications used to be conducted through human intermediaries. The role of the intermediaries can now be performed on the internet at a fraction of the cost. The internet allows you to reach a larger number of customers and suppliers in a shorter time and at a lower cost, and to conclude transactions with lower overheads in a shorter time.

---

[3] Morris, Michael, Nadler, Janice, Kurtzberg, Terri and Thompson, Leigh (1999) 'Schmooze or Lose: Communication Media, Relationship-Building, and Negotiations', Stanford GSB Research Paper #1583, October.

Most of these applications are concerned with auctions, procurement and two-party negotiations. While these are important negotiations they do tend to relate to non-relationship focused deals, so are less relevant to the preparation and thinking necessary for the type of win–win negotiating covered in this book.

Multi-party negotiations

When there are more than two parties at the table there is obviously a greater complexity, and also a greater potential for turbulence and misunderstanding. Where more people need to give and get attention at the negotiation table, the issue is likely to be more complex, there are more agendas and a greater likelihood of hidden agendas. And there is the whole issue of managing the process of who speaks, when, and how you move towards mutual agreement.

Planning and preparation

Once again, it is good to remember that no agreement is better than a bad agreement, as multi-party discussions start to exert even more pressure to make an agreement for its own sake. A good BATNA and an understanding of the costs and consequences of a failure to reach a negotiated agreement is essential.

The opening phase must include a good deal of dialogue on the form of agreement-making decisions. Will it be consensus, majority or some other form of decision? What form will the agreement take? How will the negotiation process be managed? If consideration is not given to these areas at the outset, then chaos is likely to ensue.

Managing the process

Consider appointing a chairperson, ideally a neutral party who has no stake in the negotiation. This will allow everyone to get a fair hearing, and will avoid any feeling of bias that would come from using one of the negotiators as the chairperson.

Agree the process, using the OPEC model, so that everyone knows what is expected from them at each step, what the outcomes and expectations are, and can see a clear route to a mutually acceptable agreement. The chairperson can then move the multiple parties through the action steps together.

Negotiate and agree the issues. In a multi-party negotiation there are likely to be multiple issues, so it is a good step to clarify the priority issues to be dealt with and which are of less priority (but what is of low priority to you may be of high priority to another). A good chairperson can facilitate this, but that does not absolve the parties of their responsibility to consider and discuss these openly.

Again, a good chairperson will manage the dialogue and ensure that there are appropriate agreements to deal with intolerance, emotions, inappropriate or ineffective behaviour and arguments. But that does not mean that you can avoid any responsibility yourself to agree to and work to these guidelines.

Take more breaks. In a multi-party negotiation, use more time outs to caucus with your own side, take advice and prepare. Don't wait for the chairperson to call one if you feel the need. These breaks are also great opportunities for informal dialogue and exploring alliances and mutual benefit with other parties in the negotiation.

Pay more attention to implementation pitfalls and uncertainties – when multiple parties are involved, it is easy to miss factors that can derail the implementation of an agreement.

Negotiating in a team

In studies of team negotiation, the biggest challenges come from your own side of the table. Teams must be disciplined and work together, otherwise there is always the potential for the content or relationship in a negotiation to be undermined by an inappropriate intervention from one of the team members.

One of the first requirements for a negotiating team is to align the interests. The negotiating team is likely to be rife with internal conflicts. Even though team members are all technically on the same side (they come from the same company), they often have different priorities and imagine different ideal outcomes: sales want a deal, purchasing are concerned about costs, lawyers are focused on contracts and intellectual property protection. All of these differences are potential sources of conflict and need to be resolved through negotiation before you engage with the other party.

Agree the objective of the negotiation with the other party, and the parameters that you will set. There is a matrix of interlocking issues and objectives to be addressed. Your first requirement is to negotiate on these issues and priorities to agree a common position that you will take to the negotiation with the other party. Many members of the team will be representing different constituent issues, so resolving them will require the team to focus on common ground and consider the bigger picture.

There are great advantages to teams in achieving success. Teams typically produce better results than solo negotiators, even where there is a team on one side only. Teams stimulate more discussion and more information sharing than individuals do, particularly concerning issues, interests and priorities. Teams feel more powerful and more advantaged than solo negotiators, and even under highly stressful situations team negotiators feel less competitive and pressured than do solo negotiators.

The other preparation requirements are therefore to agree roles and the process for the negotiation. It can be helpful to have different interests represented in the team so that the important decision makers and opinions are represented in real time. But there has to be agreement on how you will work together in front of the other negotiating party. A single voice is important, even if it represents a great deal of discussion and negotiation behind the scenes. So a key role of the preparation negotiations is to agree who is the leader in the negotiations and who else takes which role.

In looking for a team balance, as discussed earlier in the book, it could be useful to make sure that you have all four communication styles represented. That way you are able to have a negotiating team that can deal with every phase of the OPEC sequence effectively. Members do not necessarily have to take the lead in their strength, they can provide coaching and support to the negotiation leader to ensure that the phase is conducted effectively.

You might also consider appointing a listener and summariser in the team. It is always very useful for the negotiation leader to know that there are several eyes and ears working. It removes a lot of the stress of the lead position and makes sure that things get noticed. It is much easier to pay attention to listening for all of the signals if you do not have the responsibility to talk as well. You notice much more from an observer position than from an involved one.

Don't fall into the trap of believing that there is strength in numbers. If someone is in the negotiating team and does not have a role, be brutal and ask the question 'Why are they there?' Idle hands can make mischief. It is also a mistake to take along a team just to match the numbers on the other side. A well briefed and functioning team can perform just as well as a larger one on the other side. In the majority of instances, there will be only one or two people actively contributing during the table discussions, so everyone else is only contributing to the full in the time outs, recesses and caucuses.

Once again, the opportunity to call a recess or caucus should be exercised more frequently in a team negotiation. Teams should take advantage of opportunities to break away from the other side, whether to raise new issues, do a 'reality check' or resolve internal disputes. You can also call a caucus for strategic reasons – to speed up closure by formulating potential agreements, or slow down talks, giving both sides time to consider options and make offers. Your disengagement strategy should form part of your preparation as a team so that everyone is clear about what is happening during the negotiation.

Reviewing it

10

Reviewing your negotiation and improving your skills

In this chapter I introduce some tools for you to use when reviewing and looking back at a recent negotiation in which you have been involved:

- What went well?
- What could you improve?
- Could the outcome be better?
- What could you have done differently to get a better outcome?

I also include some development exercises and activities that you can use to develop your negotiation skills, and some tips and ideas for overcoming some of the common pitfalls and obstacles to achieving a win–win outcome in your negotiations.

Successful negotiators review their negotiations more often, and spend more time reviewing, than average negotiators. This is how they do it.

Reviewing the negotiation

There are two significant questions to pose (to both parties) after any negotiation:

1 Have you reached an agreement?

2 Are you happy with the outcome?

A key objective for entering into the negotiation is to reach an agreement. So the first question has to be 'Have you reached an agreement?'

It may sound simple and straightforward, but the answers to this question can be quite varied as they depend on each party's perception of what an agreement is, and their perception of whether they have reached that point or not. One party may believe that there is an agreement, while the other party believes that they are still negotiating:

- ▆ 'We have a deal.'
- ▆ 'We have a deal in principle, there are one or two issues to clarify before we can finalise it.'

This is one of the biggest pitfalls in the closing stage of the negotiation. The success of achieving an outcome may mean you do not pay proper attention to what the other party is saying and feeling. (The communication style used is action style, which means that listening to feelings is not important, whereas speed and outcome focus are.) If the other party is still in a negotiating mode, then you need to be there too.

The second question looks equally simple and straightforward – after all, if there is an agreement it means we are happy . . . Not necessarily. You may be happy that the agreement satisfies both parties from your perspective, but the other party may still have some reservations that they have not articulated or find it difficult to express. They may feel pressurised in some way into a compromise which, in their heart of hearts, is not one with which they are happy. They may feel as though they should have stood up for their needs more. They may feel that this deal is OK but there is probably a better one. Any of these reasons would be cause for the other party to be less than happy with the outcome, even though there is an agreement in place.

Another key objective that defines win–win negotiation is that 'all leave with a desirable result'. So it is imperative that both parties need to be happy with the outcome. If one party is not happy, then you need to re-engage. If not, then you will undoubtedly encounter difficulties with implementing the agreement (the reservations will surface later) or have difficulty in conducting a future negotiation with the other party (there will be a feeling of lose–win). It is good to remember that no agreement is better than a bad agreement.

Evaluation and feedback

Following the assessment of success based on the two initial questions, you can then further review and evaluate the quality of the negotiation. You can review the processes, strategies and tactics employed and the behaviours used during the negotiation. In reviewing, you are probably limited to your own perspective of the negotiation, unless you have a very strong partnership working relationship with the other party, with a joint desire to learn to conduct better negotiations together.

I recall that a senior manager who had attended one of my negotiation workshops invited, and paid for, a senior manager from his key supplier to attend the same workshop. His objective was to ensure that they both used the same process for negotiation which they could employ both during and after the negotiation to ensure that they got the best mutual outcome, and that they learned to improve their negotiation and relationship at each encounter. However, this is unusual and most of the time you will be reviewing on your own. If you have been working in a negotiating team then there is, of course, more than just your individual reflection, but it will be a one-sided review.

Process review

In reviewing the processes, strategies and tactics, think through what happened during the negotiation using the OPEC phases and action steps (see Figure 10.1) as your guide. The OPEC phases and action steps should be completed satisfactorily for the negotiation to be successful. Any phase or action step that is not completed effectively will have an impact on the outcome. You are, of course, only in control of your own inputs to these phases and action steps, but you do have a responsibility to help the other party to carry out the requirements and to check their satisfaction and comfort before moving on. In order to get to a win–win outcome, you may need to put effort into helping the other party put their case forward and to follow the process, especially if they are inexperienced or less skilful in negotiation. So, when you consider what you did well and what you could improve, think about the other party as well as yourself.

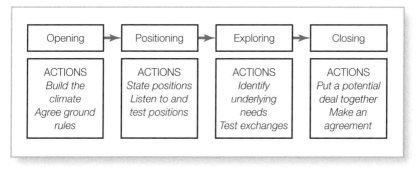

figure 10.1 The OPEC phases and actions

Opening – Build the climate

How did you greet and welcome the other party? Did you show interest in them and their organisation/business? Did you build a positive atmosphere? Did you share and listen to expectations and goals? Did you surface any issues that need to be aired? Did you focus on expressing common ground? Did you express positive expectations? Were there any issues with the location, layout and seating? Were both parties involved in the discussion? Did both parties agree to move on?

What did you do well?	What could you improve?

Tip

Successful negotiators spend longer and put more effort into building the relationship, and focus more on emphasising common ground than average negotiators.

Opening – Agree ground rules

Did you agree the issue for negotiation? If there was more than one issue, did you agree priorities and sequencing? Did you clarify an agenda? Did you agree a timetable? Did you agree the form of agreement required? Did you agree any meeting and recording protocols? Did you discuss and agree process steps (using OPEC) for the negotiation? What ground rules for productive dialogue were agreed, if any? Were both parties involved in the discussion? Did both parties agree to move on?

What did you do well?	What could you improve?

Tip

Successful negotiators clarify issues and follow agendas and meeting protocols more than average negotiators.

Positioning – State positions

Did you state your opening position clearly and concisely? Did the other party state their opening position?

What did you do well?	What could you improve?

Tip

Successful negotiators stick to their two or three strongest points and set their opening expectations higher than average negotiators.

Positioning – Listen to and test positions

Did you check the other party's opening positions for understanding? Did the other party understand your opening position? Were the opening positions tested for flexibility and potential movement? Were all facts and logic tested? Was the gap between positions identified? Were both parties involved in the discussion? Did both parties agree to move on?

What did you do well?	What could you improve?

Tip

Successful negotiators do not add more pressure or try to persuade, they move on to exploring after establishing the size of the gap.

Exploring – Identify underlying needs

Did you use reflective and probing questions? Did you use question funnelling? Did you manage to identify the other party's underlying and basic needs? Did you summarise understanding? How well/how completely did you share your own needs? Did you disclose all the information you had? Were both parties involved in the discussion? Did both parties deepen understanding? Did both parties agree to move on?

What did you do well?	What could you improve?

Tip

Successful negotiators ask significantly more questions, probe deeper, test understanding more, and summarise more frequently than average negotiators.

Exploring – Test exchanges

Did you identify alternatives? Did you identify alternatives of low cost and/or high value? Did you test out conditional exchanges? Did you ensure that you made no unilateral concessions? Were both parties involved in the discussion? Did both parties agree to move on?

What did you do well?	What could you improve?

Tip

Successful negotiators identify and use more creative alternatives than average negotiators.

Closing – Put a potential deal together

Did you identify and exchange potential deals? Did you identify and make conditional exchanges? Did you signal potential agreement? How? Did you pick up and act upon any signals of resistance from the other party? Were all loose ends tied up? Were both parties involved in the discussion? Did both parties agree to move on?

What did you do well?	What could you improve?

Tip

Successful negotiators check out all loose ends and unexpressed fears during closing, average negotiators rush to implementation.

Closing – Make an agreement

Was contracting concluded successfully? Did you write down the summary agreement? Were signatures obtained? Did you agree terms and conditions? Did you discuss, identify and resolve any implementation issues? Did you celebrate the success? Were both parties involved in the discussion? Did both parties agree to move on?

What did you do well?	What could you improve?

Tip

Successful negotiators ensure the clarity of a written and signed agreement more than average negotiators.

In reviewing the interaction phase using the OPEC model, some other process review questions will emerge.

Planning

How well did you prepare? Were all planning steps covered? Were any issues identified during the negotiation that should have been anticipated? Were the right people involved in the planning? Were all stakeholder interests identified? Was the issue clear? Were all negotiating parties identified? Was research on the other party done? Were wants, needs and haves identified? Was the other party's perspective considered?

What did you do well?	What could you improve?

Tip

Successful negotiators plan more and consider the situation from the other party's perspective more than average negotiators.

Strategy

Was the power balance correctly identified? Was the choice of negotiation strategy correct? Were goals and expectations identified? Was you opening correctly positioned? Were your limits identified correctly? Were alternatives and options identified? Did you identify your BATNA? Was the other party's perspective considered?

What did you do well?	What could you improve?

Tip

Successful negotiators consider a wider range of options and outcomes, especially those that might be raised by the other party.

Taking time-outs and breaks

Did you plan a time-out strategy? Did you take time outs when needed? Did you offer the other party breaks?

What did you do well?	What could you improve?

Tip

Successful negotiators take more breaks than average negotiators.

Using time efficiently

The time spent in the negotiation needs to be appropriate for the importance of the negotiation. Was the time spent in the interaction right? Could you have spent longer? Did you spend too long? Was time used efficiently? Did the other party find the time well spent?

What did you do well?	What could you improve?

Tip

Spending longer does not necessarily bring added value.

Negotiation medium

Was it a face-to-face, telephone, email or internet negotiation? Was the right medium used? How could you use it better? Would a different medium be more effective or efficient? Was the cost and time investment right?

What did you do well?	What could you improve?

Tip

Efficiency is not the same as effectiveness.

Negotiation team

Was a team used? Were the interests aligned? Were the roles clear?
Was everyone needed? Did you agree a process? Could the planning
phase be improved? Could the interaction phase be improved? How
did the team work together?

What did you do well?	What could you improve?

Tip

Successful negotiators are willing to use other's expertise and
recognise that a team might be valuable in a negotiation.

Cross-cultural issues

Were there cross-cultural issues? Were these identified in preparation? Were they as predicted? Were you culturally sensitive? Did issues emerge? Were you surprised? What is your new understanding?

What did you do well?	What could you improve?

Tip

Successful negotiators are culturally aware and inquisitive.

Behaviour review

You will recall from Chapter 6 that each of the OPEC phases has a communication style associated with it that will ensure that the process steps are conducted effectively (see Figure 10.2). So it is also possible to reflect on the negotiation interaction and identify where you were effective and what areas you could improve the outcome of by developing a greater skill in the communication style.

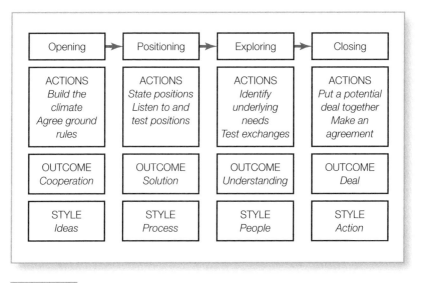

figure 10.2 The OPEC phases, action steps and communication styles

Ideas style

Used as the primary style in opening and as a secondary style in exploring. There are two behaviours involved:

1 Connecting – identifying and articulating areas of commonality in ideas, thoughts, experiences, expectations, beliefs and values. The deeper the connection the more collaboration and cooperation can be expected.

2 Envisioning – talking about what you can do together, focusing on future possibilities. Positive outlook, stating expectations for success and future cooperation.

What did you do well?	What could you improve?

Tip

Successful negotiators focus more on areas of commonality and spend more time building positive relationships for the future.

Process style

The primary style in positioning. There are two behaviours involved:

1 Proposing – making proposals and suggestions. Stating your opening position.

2 Reasoning – supporting proposals with data and logical argument to support your opening. Using logic and reasoning to argue against others' suggestions and opening to test them.

What did you do well?	What could you improve?

Tip

Successful negotiators make clear and concise proposals and limit themselves to the most important two or three points.

People style

Used as the primary style in exploring and as a secondary style in opening. There are two behaviours involved:

1 Sharing – sharing your feelings and disclosing information. Disclosing your underlying needs and possible alternative exchanges.

2 Listening – asking questions, summarising and checking to establish understanding. Encouraging deeper sharing around feelings, beliefs and values. Identifying underlying needs. Developing empathetic understanding. Listening carefully to alternative exchanges.

What did you do well?	What could you improve?

Tip

Successful negotiators ask significantly more questions, probe deeper, test understanding more, summarise more frequently and work with more creative alternatives.

Action style

The primary style in closing. There are two behaviours involved:

1 Demanding – saying exactly what you want.

2 Exchanging – offering exchanges in return for what you want. Putting the deal together so that both parties gets what they want.

What did you do well?	What could you improve?

Tip

Successful negotiators focus on the balance of the deal and the outcome.

If you are working as part of a negotiating team, then you can give each other feedback on the use of communication styles during the negotiation. If you are working solo, then you will need to reflect on how well you used each behaviour and what potential there is to improve. Your own personal preferences for the style will probably have an impact on your assessment. You will perceive greater opportunities for improvement in the styles where you are less comfortable. However, this may obscure the potential for improvement in the other styles. Just because you are comfortable in the style does not mean you are effective. Think about what you did well in each style, and what you could improve in each as well.

Improving your negotiation skill

Planning and preparation

Use the checklists and planning guides outlined in Chapters 3, 5 and 6. These checklists and guides will help you to make a comprehensive plan for the negotiation.

Working as a team and using experts at the planning stage will improve the negotiation outcome. Planning is best done from as many perspectives as possible. Successful negotiators plan carefully, know the product/project they are working on, understand the rules and the alternatives, and have the courage to probe and check information from as many sources as needed. They make sure that there are no gaps that can spring a surprise during the negotiation. They also spend more time thinking about the negotiation from the other party's perspective and consider a wider range of options and outcomes during the planning phase. They can do this more successfully if they are working together with other people who know the situation and the other party.

Having completed the plan to the best standard in the appropriate time, the biggest potential for improvement in the preparation phase will come from rehearsing the negotiation. Put your plan into action with someone else (or another team if it is a team negotiation) taking the role of the other party. You are conducting a dress rehearsal. In the rehearsal, you can check out which alternatives might work best; where you might wish to spend longer; where you could speed up.

You can also check your assumptions and behaviours by getting the people playing the role of the other party to act differently to what you might predict. This will increase your flexibility. You can also rehearse the moves through the OPEC phases, and practise your time-out strategies. The learning you will get from this rehearsal step will more than pay off the time investment.

One big word of caution: the objective of the rehearsal is to test out your plan and build confidence in your behaviours and preparation. It is not to create a plan that is foolproof. There is no such thing. A plan is just that – a plan. You cannot predict what will happen in the actual negotiation, so too much preparation is dangerous – unless that preparation has focused on different scenarios which allow you to be flexible in responding to what emerges on the day.

Developing communication styles[1]

Action style

■ Find someone with whom to practise, and get feedback. (Ideally someone who has a preference for the action style as they can give you feedback on what is most effective for them.)

■ Ask them to help you using action style. Make a clear **demand** about what you want them to do. Tell them exactly what you will do for them in **exchange**.

■ Role play different situations with them where you will need to use action style in real life negotiations.

  – Ask them to take the role of someone from whom you need some information but who does not work directly for you. **Demand** from this person that they give you the information you need. Tell them what you want and exactly what you will do for them in **exchange**.

  – Ask them to take the role of your boss. **Demand** from your boss that they allow you to take full responsibility for a project. Offer an **exchange** in return.

  – Ask them to take the role of your boss. **Demand** from your boss that they give you a salary increase. Offer an **exchange** to complete the deal.

■ Get feedback from your partner on how you can improve your content and style, paying particular attention to the words, music and dance.

Process style

■ Find someone with whom to practise, and get feedback. (Ideally someone who has a preference for the process style as they can give you feedback on what is most effective for them.)

---

[1] The four communication styles are described in more detail in Cox, Geof (2010) *Getting Results Without Authority: The new rules of organisational influence*, BookShaker.com. Details of training courses are available at **www.gettingresultswithoutauthority.com**

- Use process style to get them to practise with you. **Propose** that your partner works with you. Use no more than two **reasons** to justify your proposal. Your partner can resist if your reasoning is not sound.
- Ask your partner to take the role of the other party in a negotiation. Make your opening position statement where you need to use process style.
  - **Propose** that your boss allows you to attend a three-week training course in the USA. Use no more than three **reasons** in support.
  - Make a **proposal** to a supplier to your organisation. Support your proposal with data and logical **reasoning**.
  - Make a **proposal** to form a partnership relationship with your organisation. Support your proposal with logical **reasoning**.
- Get feedback from your partner on how you can improve your content and style, paying particular attention to the words, music and dance.

People style

- Find someone with whom to practise, and get feedback. (Ideally someone who has a preference for the people style as they can give you feedback on what is most effective for them.)
- Use people style to get them to practise with you. **Share** your feelings and needs, and ask for help. Invite their response and **listen** in order to understand their feelings and reactions to your needs.
- Ask your partner to take the role of the other party in a real life negotiation. Use people style to understand the motivations and needs of the other party.
  - **Share** the underlying drivers and needs that you must have satisfied. Invite the other party to share their motivations and needs and **listen** actively in order to understand.
  - Ask your partner to disclose their expectations for a negotiation. **Share** your motivations for the request. **Listen** by asking probing questions and summarising to discover their underlying motivations and values in negotiating. **Share** your motivations and values in negotiating and explore the differences. (People style is about listening to understand, you do not have to agree.)
- Get feedback from your partner on how you can improve your content and style, paying particular attention to the words, music and dance

Ideas style

■ Find someone with whom to practise, and get feedback. (Ideally someone who has a preference for the ideas style as they can give you feedback on what is most effective for them.)

■ Use ideas style to get them to practise with you. Share what you see as the ideas, experiences, values and beliefs you have in common to establish a **connection**. **Envision** the potential of working together.

■ Ask your partner to take the role of the other party in a real life negotiation. Use ideas style to build a positive climate and envision a successful outcome to the negotiation.

   – Articulate what you see as the **connection** that binds you together and share your **vision** for the outcome of the negotiation.

■ Get feedback from your partner on how you can improve your content and style, paying particular attention to the words, music and dance.

Summary

Win–win negotiation is an interactive process where two or more parties with common and conflicting interests come together to exchange ideas and propositions in order to reach an agreement where they all leave with a desirable result, after fully taking into account each others' interests.

By having a collaborative and positive mindset, and using the process and behavioural tools in this book, you will have more successful and more satisfying negotiations in your business life (or in your personal relationships).

By using the reviewing tools in this chapter and taking the time to reflect on each negotiation you undertake, you will build your skills and expertise and have even more successful negotiations. Successful win–win negotiation is a journey, not a destination. Every negotiation is different and unique, so the challenge is always new and exciting. I wish you every success in developing your skills, competence and confidence.

Glossary of terms

Although many of the terms in use in this book may be familiar to readers, some may not be as well known, so a glossary of some of the negotiation concepts and terms used in the book are included here for reference:

Action style   A style of communicating where people are task -oriented, keen to get things done, decisive and direct. They bargain with people to get a deal. (*See also* Ideas, Process and People styles.)

BATNA   An acronym for Best Alternative to a Negotiated Agreement described by Roger Fisher and William Ury in their book *Getting to Yes*. The alternative action that you can take should your proposed agreement with another party be unsuccessful. It increases your power balance and avoids the danger of making a bad deal.

Bargaining zone   The range in which an agreement is satisfactory to both parties involved in the negotiation. The bargaining zone is the overlap area between the walk away positions of both parties.

Caucus   A private, closed meeting involving one side of the negotiation with their advisers. (*See also* Recess.)

Collective bargaining   A negotiation between employers and a trade union (or other representative body) to agree conditions of employment (wages, hours of work, etc.). Normally resulting in a written contract with a specific time duration.

Common ground   The area of agreement between all parties to a negotiation that allows the discussion of areas of conflict.

Compromise   An agreement where both parties give up some of their goals and wishes in return for similar concessions from the other side, ending up at a point where both parties are equally unhappy.

Concession   The areas that you are prepared to give up (concede) that will be traded for concessions from the other party.

Cross-functional team   A group of people with different functional expertise working toward a common goal. For instance a cross-functional team may include people from finance, marketing, operations and human resources departments. It may include employees from all levels of an organisation. Cross-functional teams often function best when responding to broad, rather than specific directives, such as corporate strategy and direction. They tend to respond to consensus decision making rather than hierarchical. (*See also* Matrix management.)

Dirty tricks   Manipulative and potentially underhand methods used by negotiators to gain an unfair advantage over other parties (as perceived by the receiver). (*See also* Tactics.)

Distributive negotiation   A negotiation process that normally entails only a single issue, often price. Also referred to as a 'fixed pie' negotiation because one party generally gains at the expense of another party. Distributive negotiation often ends in a compromise agreement which does not fully satisfy either party.

Haggling   A simple form of distributive negotiation. To negotiate, argue or barter about the terms of a business transaction, usually focusing on the purchase or selling price of a product or service.

Ideas style   A style of communicating where people use their responsiveness to connect with other people's values and beliefs and build exciting possibilities for the future. They inspire people to cooperate with each other. (*See also* Action, Process and People styles.)

Influence   Using personal power to get someone to do something, whist maintaining or building a positive working relationship.

Lose–lose   A negotiation result where all parties to a negotiation leave the negotiation unhappy, having not achieved their needs. (*See also* Win–lose and Win–win.)

Matrix management   A type of organisational management in which people with similar skills are pooled for work assignments. For example, all IT specialists may be in one IT department and report to an IT manager, but these same specialists may be assigned to one or more different projects and report to a project manager(s) while working on that project. Therefore, each specialist has reporting lines to several managers.

Matrix organisation   A organisation structure where reporting lines are drawn with respect to geography, function, products or other differences. The matrix may be stronger in one dimension than the other, usually depicted by having 'dotted line' relationships versus 'straight line' relationships – the straight line usually taking precedence – or they may be balanced where there is no priority.

Multi-party negotiation   A negotiation that involves more than two parties.

Non-verbal communication   The process of sending and receiving wordless messages through: gesture, body language, posture, facial expression and eye contact; speech elements such as voice quality, emotion, pace, rhythm, intonation and stress.

Negotiation   An interactive process between two or more parties seeking to find common ground on an issue or issues of mutual interest or dispute where the involved parties seek to make or find a mutually acceptable agreement that will be honoured by all the parties concerned.

Negotiation strategy   A strategic approach to the negotiation that guides the negotiating behaviour throughout. The strategic decision is based on an assessment of the current and future relationship between the parties.

OPEC   The acronym formed from the initial letters of the four phases of interaction: Opening, Positioning, Exploring and Closing.

Opening position   The starting point for a negotiation. A statement of a desired result from one party that will meet their interests in the conflict.

People style   A style of communicating where people are responsive to others' needs and use their listening and sharing skills to build team working, synergy and shared understanding. They build empathy with people to build understanding. (*See also* Action, Process and Ideas styles.)

Principled negotiation   An approach that helps negotiators to find a mutually shared outcome, a win–win outcome, by avoiding some of the pitfalls of positional bargaining. First identified in *Getting to Yes* by Fisher and Ury.

Process style   A style of communicating where people are task focused but not directive or forceful, relying on logical and rational argument. They debate to find a solution. (*See also* Action, Ideas and People styles.)

Project organisation   Another name for a matrix organisation structure that is defined in one dimension by a number of different projects. (*See also* Matrix management, Matrix organisation.)

Recess   A meeting called by one or both of the parties in the negotiation to discuss responses, strategies and tactics in private. (*See also* Caucus.)

Reciprocation   Making an exchange of something in return for something given by another party.

Reframing   Seeing a situation in another context that lets go of limiting beliefs from one view and set of assumptions, allowing new conception and interpretation possibilities to develop.

Remote team   A work team that is geographically dispersed and meets face-to-face infrequently or not at all. The team members may be in different locations in the same country or scattered around the world, linked through telephone and electronic communications media. (*See also* Virtual team.)

Stakeholder   Someone who has an interest or a stake in the outcome of a negotiation, project, event or organisation.

Stakeholder mapping/analysis   A process where all the individuals or groups that are likely to be affected by a proposed action are identified and then sorted according to how much they can affect the action and how much the action can affect them. This information is analysed to assess how the interests of those stakeholders should be addressed in a plan.

Tactics   The methods used by negotiators to gain an advantage over other parties. Tactics are often deceptive and manipulative and are used to fulfil one party's goals and objectives – often to the detriment of the other negotiation parties. (*See also* Dirty tricks.)

Virtual team   A group of individuals who work across time, space, and organisational boundaries with links strengthened by webs of communication technology. They typically have complementary skills and are committed to a common purpose. Members of virtual teams communicate electronically, so they may never meet face-to-face. Many virtual teams consist of employees both working at home and in small groups in the different geographic offices. (*See also* Remote team.)

Walk away   The point at which a negotiator will leave the negotiation as the offer from the other side does not meet their lowest acceptable position.

Win–lose   A distributive negotiation whereby one party's gain is another party's loss.

Win–win   Win–win negotiation is an interactive process where two or more parties who have both common and conflicting interests come together to exchange ideas and propositions in order to reach an agreement where they all leave with a desirable result, after fully taking into account each others' interests.

Words, music and dance   A shorthand description of the elements of face-to-face communication covering the literal meaning of the verbal message (words), the tone and non-verbal messages in the voice (music) and the non-verbal messages in the gestures and body language (dance).

ZOPA   An acronym that stands for Zone of Possible Agreement. It is the range or area in which an agreement is satisfactory to both parties involved in the negotiation process. (*See also* Bargaining zone.)

Index

FINANCIAL TIMES
Essential Guides

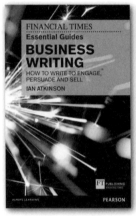

9780273761136

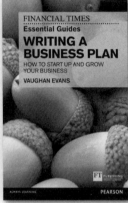

9780273757986

9780273757993

9780273768135

9780273772217

9780273772422

Available to buy online and from all good bookshops
www.pearson-books.com